Archival
Choices

The LexingtonBooks Special Series in Libraries and Librarianship

Richard D. Johnson, General Editor

The Parliament of Great Britain: A Bibliography
Robert U. Goehlert and *Fenton S. Martin*

Prizewinning Books for Children
Jaqueline Shachter Weiss

The Feminization of Librarianship in France
Mary Niles Maack

The Public Library in the 1980s
Lawrence J. White

International Business Reference Sources
Cynthia C. Ryans

Vietnam War Bibliography
Christopher L. Sugnet and *John Hickey*

The Electronic Library
Hugh F. Cline and *Loraine T. Sinnott*

Archival Choices
Nancy E. Peace

Contracts, RFPs, and other Procurement Documents for Library Automation
Edwin M. Cortez

Archival Choices

Managing the Historical Record in an Age of Abundance

Edited by
Nancy E. Peace
Simmons College

Lexington Books
D.C. Heath and Company
Lexington, Massachusetts
Toronto

Library of Congress Cataloging in Publication Data
Main entry under title:

Archival choices.

Bibliography: p.
Includes index.
1. Archives—United States—Administration—Addresses, essays,
lectures.   I. Peace, Nancy E.
CD3021.A79   1984   0.25.17'14'0973   81-48395
ISBN 0-669-05354-6

Copyright © 1984 by D.C. Heath and Company

Published simultaneously in Canada

Printed in the United States of America

International Standard Book Number: 0-669-05354-6

Library of Congress Catalog Card Number: 81-48395

Contents

Foreword

Publications written by outstanding practitioners that contribute to the development of theoretical concepts are doubly welcome. Not only are the authors schooled firmly in the day-to-day realities of practicing their profession, and thus to be heeded, but also they are able to use their experience to raise the level of discussion and to articulate the principles that guide their work. This is such a publication, and, thus, it is doubly welcome to archivists and others who care about modern records.

Within the archivist's overall dual responsibilities of preserving and making available for use the records in his care, the functional area of records appraisal and disposition is central to his work. This area, which includes all actions taken with respect to records that determine their ultimate fate, whether it be temporary storage, permanent preservation, reproduction in another form, or outright destruction, is the heart of the archival profession. But the questions raised in this area and the solutions proposed are not always universally applicable or acceptable. Within the past year, for example, the National Archives and Records Service has created a major task force to look again at the appraisal process, and a major private foundation has funded a program at the University of Michigan for archival scholars to focus on this issue. This book, which places major emphasis on appraisal from a variety of perspectives, contributes information and ideas to the discussion of this important issue.

Nancy E. Peace was stimulated to prepare this book by a conference held at the National Archives's John F. Kennedy Library. Beginning with the papers presented at the conference, she has gone on to assemble a talented and thoughtful group of writers to discuss records disposition in its broadest theoretical and practical aspects, including appraisal, the role of records management, and deaccessioning.

Not all readers will accept the positions expounded in this book, but that is not the intent of the work. As the editor points out, the volume is designed to stimulate discussion, research, and publication on these important questions. Similarly, despite the high level of work, not all of the provocative topics that are covered will be equally useful to each reader. But I am sure all thoughtful archivists will welcome this book as a useful and stimulating contribution to the archival literature of the 1980s.

Robert M. Warner

Preface

The idea for this book grew out of a workshop on processing contemporary collections held at Boston's John F. Kennedy Library in 1980. Organized by Helen W. Slotkin, institute archivist, Massachusetts Institute of Technology, this gathering of approximately thirty invited participants brought together archivists, curators, and librarians from institutions as diverse as M.I.T. and the American Antiquarian Society. Participants described how collections are processed in their own institutions, with the aim of discovering common problems and exploring potential solutions. On the whole, it was a productive day, although many people left feeling that they had learned more about problems than solutions.

While workshops are a useful means of sharing information and examining problems, their transient nature means that the ideas and information presented are neither widely shared nor permanently recorded. Consequently, John Dojka and I agreed that what was needed was a publication that would focus on problems of processing contemporary records. Our goals were to: (1) describe archival practice in selected institutions; (2) examine current archival theory in light of the particular problems presented by contemporary records; and (3) stimulate new research and writing, whether along lines suggested by the contributors or in opposition to them.

Because appraisal seemed to be the most difficult problem facing processors of twentieth-century collections, the book initially was to have focused on this narrow aspect of processing. As chapters began to arrive, however, it quickly became apparent that broader issues had to be addressed. In particular, Philip N. Cronenwett's chapter on appraisal of literary manuscripts makes clear that issues of deaccessioning and selling cannot be ignored. It was fortunate that, just as we were discussing how best to address these issues, we became aware of Lawrence Dowler's paper on deaccessioning, which he had prepared for the Spring 1982 meeting of New England Archivists and which focuses on the very questions we believed needed consideration and also raises a few that had not occurred to us. Similarly, F. Gerald Ham, in a paper presented to the 1982 Society of American Archivists meeting, addresses a number of issues raised by other authors. More important, his paper takes a broad perspective and ties together the very themes we were attempting to address. The addition of these two authors' chapters gives the book balance and symmetry.

Because of the nature of the subject, no attempt was made to produce a book that was comprehensive or definitive. Rather, contributors were selected because their work appeared to have developed along lines that the Kennedy Library workshop revealed were the concerns of the profession. We sought diversity of subject focus and methodological approach. Thus, authors Patricia Aronsson and Philip N. Cronenwett describe their analyses of contemporary records produced by two types of individuals—congressmen and literary authors—and offer specific recommendations regarding appraisal and processing. John Dojka focuses on the records of an institution—Yale University—in order to advocate a particular methodological approach to processing all college and university records. Francis X. Blouin, Jr., examines the diverse nature of business documentation and concludes that processing and appraisal methods must be developed for particular industries or types of businesses. As previously noted, Lawrence Dowler discusses deaccessioning, and F. Gerald Ham outlines a program for managing records in the 1980s and beyond. The first chapter describes the evolution of appraisal theory and methodology.

Several contributors identify questions they believe need further investigation. It is hoped that this book will stimulate not only discussion but also research and publication. Hard data, thoughtful analysis, and vigorous self-criticism will be needed if archivists are to be adequately prepared to meet the demands of the coming decades.

Acknowledgments

I gratefully acknowledge the many people who contributed to the publication of this book. First are the colleagues who worked so hard and so enthusiastically on the individual chapters. Without them there would be no book. Special thanks are owed F. Gerald Ham, for providing a title that expresses the book's theme with clarity and style. Sten Lofgren, M.D., kindly took on the substantial project of translating the relevant chapter in Nils Nilsson's book for a person he had never met. Without Dr. Lofgren's effort, this important author might have remained largely unknown in this country. Michael Winship, editor of the *Bibliography of American Literature*, translated from the German the summary of Hans Booms's thoughtful paper on appraisal theory and contributed many useful insights regarding the work of both Nilsson and Booms. Megan Sniffin-Marinoff, archivist of Simmons College, Professor Leigh Estabrook of Syracuse University, and Michael Winship read drafts of chapter 1. Their many constructive comments were greatly appreciated. Billie Lawrence and Catherine M. Leary worked under the pressure of a short deadline to produce the final typed copy. Their diligence and good humor exceeded reasonable expectations. Finally, I wish to acknowledge the patience and continuing support of Marjorie A. Glazer, Jaime Welch, and Mike McCarroll of Lexington Books. Despite missed deadlines and disappearing authors, they seemed never to doubt that this book would be completed.

1

Deciding What to Save: Fifty Years of Theory and Practice

Nancy E. Peace

The Nature of Contemporary Records

For the past fifty years, archivists throughout the world have sought to articulate some model or set of criteria that would guide them in the difficult task of determining which records, among the vast number produced each year, shall be preserved for posterity. To date, no single model or set of guidelines has emerged. Different authors have focused on different aspects of the problem—some exploring the philosophical bases of appraisal, some the techniques for implementing appraisal decisions.[1] Underlying all their work, however, is the recognition that the amount and complexity of twentieth-century documentation present a special challenge to archivists.

A maxim of contemporary archival lore is that older collections tend to be smaller and proportionately richer than more recent ones. The reasons are many and well-known. Perhaps foremost in determining the size and content of twentieth-century collections has been the development of modern technology. On the one hand, it has changed the means by which people communicate, thereby altering the records they produce. Telephones, computers, and air travel now permit communications that once were possible only through written correspondence. The record of these communications is lost or preserved only in the diminished, subjective form of a participant's notes or recollections. On the other hand, because of the ease with which material can be reproduced through photocopying, microfilming, and computing, modern technology has led to a greater physical bulk of records that are retained.

The organization of modern life also affects the quantity and quality of the records that many societies, especially industrial and postindustrial ones, generate. When Robert M. Warner, archivist of the United States, was director of the Michigan Historical Collections in Ann Arbor, he took great delight in contrasting the twelve feet of neatly arranged papers belonging to Henry Howland Crapo, governor of Michigan in the 1860s, with the more than five-hundred feet of George W. Romney's records, then being processed in the basement of a nearby university building. The records produced by the executive of a government serving the needs of approximately 700,000 inhabitants were considerably fewer than those produced

1

by the executive of a government serving more than 7 million people. Analogous developments have occurred in nearly all modern organizations, from universities to businesses.

The increased bulk of contemporary records has changed the nature of the archivist's job. In the 1840s, Lyman Draper, first director of the State Historical Society of Wisconsin, could travel over half the Midwest searching out papers with little fear of being overwhelmed by his acquisitions, while today's archivists must be ever mindful of the vast amounts of documentation that are candidates for preservation.[2] The need to select what shall be preserved, to separate the chaff from the wheat, means that the archivist can no longer be simply a preserver but, as Canadian archivist W. Kay Lamb has noted, must be a destroyer as well.[3] The dilemma posed by this more complex role is: How shall the archivist determine what shall be destroyed? The decision to destroy a record, once carried out, is irrevocable. Writing in 1962, Lamb urged his colleagues to recognize the destroyer aspect of their jobs so that they could carry out this function in a sane and responsible fashion. Citing Canada's Public Records Committee as an example of how destruction can be controlled bureaucratically, Lamb argued for the systematic advanced planning of records retention and destruction so as to avoid the need to make ill-considered decisions in the face of a crisis. Established in 1945, the Public Records Committee administers Canada's records-management program.

Over a period of years, the U.S. government also developed policies for administering a records program. The National Archives Act of 1934 not only established the National Archives as a government agency, but charged that agency to acquire, preserve, and make available for research official records of enduring value. While this legislation constituted a major advance in the government's effort to establish a federal records program, it focused primarily on the preservation of records and gave the archives staff only an advisory role regarding the disposal of no longer valuable records. Only Congress could authorize the destruction of records. The Records Disposal Act of 1939 expanded the authority of the archivist somewhat, giving him limited power to authorize destruction of records when Congress was not in session. According to Donald R. McCoy, National Archives chronicler, of particular significance was the act's approval of "the development of schedules of disposable records so that records of the same kind that Congress had previously authorized for disposition could be so identified that they could be destroyed without legislative approval when Congress was not in session."[4] The agency's records-disposal authority was further enhanced in 1943, when Congress passed the Act Concerning the Disposal of Records. One of its more significant provisions was authorization for the preparation of disposal schedules for specified kinds of records in an agency. Unwanted records could be destroyed automatically once Congress had approved the schedule. A 1945 amendment permitted preparation of schedules covering similar records in two or more agencies.

The concept of a full-scale records-management program for federal agencies was finally recognized with passage of the Federal Records Act in 1950. By this time, the National Archives had been subsumed under the General Services Administration (GSA) as the National Archives and Records Service (NARS). The act pulled together most of the previous legislation relating to the National Archives and expanded the authority and responsibility of GSA and NARS. It also provided for the creation of a network of regional records centers that would accept records of federal agencies operating outside of Washington. As a result of legislative mandates, the NARS staff has instituted various programs to enable the service to meet its records-control responsibilities. The early programs were modest because both the scope of the task was unknown and the authority of the agency was limited. Over the years, the agency's authority has been expanded as federal offficials and Congress have come to recognize the magnitude of the records-control problem. Few would argue, however, that the National Archives has achieved an ideal level of control. The extent and variety of records generated by federal agencies in the United States continue to challenge the intellectual, physical, and financial resources of the agency. State and local governments face similar problems on a smaller scale.

Canada and the United States are not alone in recognizing the need for carefully planned records-destruction programs. Governments throughout the world have developed legislation and records-control programs in an effort to preserve their valuable records while ensuring that expensive storage space and staff time are not wasted on records of little or no value. In a paper presented to the Third International Congress of Archives in 1956, British archivist J.H. Collingridge described the records-management programs that various countries had developed to handle what D.L. Evans termed "the alarming rate of accumulation of modern state papers."[5] He found the methods of control and the principles of selecting documents for preservation remarkably similar, although there were differences in implementation and degree of program sophistication. Twenty years later, Swedish archivist Åke Kromnow, reporting on the results of another survey, informed delegates to the Seventh International Congress that most responding countries had developed retention and disposal schedules, but they were experiencing difficulties developing objective standards of appraisal, especially for nonroutine material. He noted a tremendous interest in records appraisal, which he attributed to concern about the economic consequences of the flood of contemporary records.[6]

The problem of bulk is not limited to government records. Universities, churches, businesses, civic and fraternal organizations, and individuals generate and accumulate substantial quantities of records. Like their colleagues in government, archivists responsible for nongovernmental records face considerable pressure to reduce bulk while ensuring the preservation of important records. In their 1948 report to the American Historical Association, members of the association's Ad Hoc Committee on Manuscripts observed that, while every record is potentially useful to someone at some-time, many are not of sufficient value to warrant the time it would take the archivist to process them or the researcher to use them. The committee noted that later collections, especially those produced after 1900, present more problems than did earlier collections. With later collections in particu-lar, what is needed is a sense of proportion. The archivist "must be wise enough, and bold enough, to take a calculated risk, and . . . the historian and the biographer must recognize the difficulties, assist with conference and advice whenever possible, and finally accept the situation."[7]

In the years since 1948, collections have become larger, the need for selection greater, and the issues more complex. While computers and other forms of high technology may reduce or eliminate the problems of physical bulk, it seems likely that storage and computer costs, as well as data-access constraints, will prevent archivists from divesting themselves of their selec-tion responsibilities.

As this chapter will demonstrate, many archivists have written about both the problems they have encountered in their attempt to carry out the selection task and the solutions they have identified. These authors have focused on two general themes—the philosophical basis for evaluation of materials for selection and techniques for implementing selection decision. The remaining chapters in this book address these same two themes.

Developing Programs and Standards: The Role of the National Archives of the United States

Although federal, state, and local archives have been specifically excluded from the scope of this book, the publications of the staff of the United States National Archives constitute the logical starting point for any discussion of contemporary appraisal theory and practice.[8] The work of archivists such as Philip C. Brooks, Herman Kahn, and Theodore Schellenberg are the foun-dation upon which new generations of archivists must build.

In a paper read before the Society of American Archivists in April 1940, Philip C. Brooks, then staff member of the Division of Independent Agen-cies Archives of the National Archives, attempted to describe criteria that archivists might use to identify records of "permanent value."[9] He began by noting that, before applying value criteria, archivists can substantially reduce the volume of records merely by weeding out copies. Furthermore, one document may duplicate the information contained in another. When one series of documents contains the same or substantially the same information as another series one or more series of documents can be eliminated. Accounting records are often cited as an example of information duplication, but other types of records, such as census data and personnel records, are also replicated, aggregated, and summarized.

Once duplicates are eliminated, selection can begin. Brooks urged archivists to consider three values when selecting records for permanent retention: (1) the value that the records may have for the agency that created them; (2) their usefulness for the study of adminstrative history; and (3) their historical value. In speaking of records' value to their agency of origin, Brooks meant whether the agency needs them for efficient administration and for protection against legal and other claims—the value, then, refers to the ongoing organizational function of the records. By administrative history, on the other hand, he meant utility "to later administrators seeking precedents, to political scientists or other outsiders who want to study the agency's operations, and to the archivist, who must preserve the agency's records strictly in accordance with the functions they reflect."[10] His discussion of historical value was less developed, but Brooks did admonish his colleagues not to take too narrow a view of what constituted the field of history. Too often, he remarked, people think of historical records as those individual documents that have obvious historical significance, such as treaties, letters of presidents, and the Declaration of Independence. History, however, is more than political and national developments. Indeed, "most records having historical value possess such value not as individual documents but as groups of documents that, considered altogether, reflect the activities of some organization or person or portray everyday, rather than unique, events and conditions."[11]

Brooks recognized that the archivist cannot function alone, that he needs the cooperation and assistance of staff members in the agencies for whose records he is responsible. Noting that today's records are tomorrow's archives, he urged his colleagues to take an interest in the documents from the moment they are created. He encouraged archivists to work with agency staff in developing filing schemes that would serve, not only the administrative needs of the agency, but the archival uses to which the records would be put later on. He also argued for the periodic transfer of some files to the archives, the planned destruction of others, and the possibility of temporary storage for others. In a subsequent article for *Indian Archives*, Brooks noted that the success of an ongoing records-selection program depends on the informed cooperation of records creators and administrators. He recommended that archivists explain their goals and programs in public administration journals as well as in archives literature.[12] In the speech he gave in 1940, Brooks foresaw the use of microfilm and representative sampling in the selection process, but he did not discuss these techniques at length.

While Brooks's ideas and recommendations must seem commonplace to today's archivists, in 1940 he and his colleagues were breaking new ground. In the version of his paper published in the *American Archivist*, he noted that the idea of continuous attention to the problems of selection from the beginning through the end of the life of given bodies of records had not, to his knowledge, previously been expounded at length.[13]

In his discussion of techniques for administering a sound archival program, it seems likely that Brooks drew, in part, upon the work of a National Archives colleague, Emmett J. Leahy. Leahy had conducted a survey of European archival policies, which in 1937 he had submitted to the Society of American Archivists as part of a report of the Committee on the Reduction of Archival Material. He subsequently used this data as the basis for a comparison of U.S. and European government archival practices and, as a result of his analysis, proposed a twelve-point program for the reduction of government records.[14] Incorporated in this proposed program were the concepts of archivist-administrator cooperation in selection, design of records-control systems written for each agency to facilitate segregation and expedite elimination of nonpermanent records, and utilization of microfilming and scientific sampling. Leahy's proposals addressed only the technical aspects of a records-appraisal program. He did not suggest criteria for evaluating records for permanent preservation.

In a paper prepared for the National Archives Open Conference on Administration, held in 1944, G. Philip Bauer, staff member in the Division of Labor Department Archives, advocated a pragmatic, and no doubt controversial, approach to records appraisal. Asserting that "stern and true cost accounting is a prerequisite of all orderly appraisal," Bauer articulated four categories of government records use: (1) official reference by government agencies; (2) protection of citizens' private rights; (3) serious research by scholars; and (4) satisfaction of genealogical and antiquarian curiosity. Higher costs can be justified for organizing and preserving records in the first two categories than in the final two, he argued.[15]

Bauer's paper was published two years later as number 13 in the National Archives Staff Information Circulars. Accompanying it was a summary of comments made by his colleague, Herman Kahn, then chief of the Division of Interior Department Archives. Kahn accused Bauer of believing "that the business of keeping records should be viewed in a purely commerical light—that it should play precisely the same role in our lives as the purchase of a pair of shoes."[16] While acknowledging the role of utilitarian and dollar values in records preservation, he argued that these are not the primary consideration. "We keep records because we are civilized men and therefore must do so," Kahn asserted.[17] He also accused Bauer of falling into the trap of believing that if archivists could develop a rigid set of criteria, principles, and formulas, all appraisers would evaluate the same records in the same way. Kahn thought this unlikely, because people are profoundly different and will, therefore, make profoundly different choices. He viewed these differences as healthy and expressed the hope that the National Archives would never adhere to rigid appraisal formulas, because "lack of an extremely rigid definition of policy makes possible experimentation, independent thought, change—and change means life."[18]

In 1956, another National Archives staff member, Theodore Schellenberg, attempted to describe the appraisal standards that had, by then, evolved at the National Archives.[19] His description focused on the concepts of "evidential" and "informational" value, values that he noted were implicit in the Records Disposal Act of 1939. By evidential value, Schellenberg meant the evidence public records may contain of the functioning and organization of the government body that produced them and the importance of the matter for the organization's current and future functioning. Informational value referred to the information the records might contain on any persons, corporate bodies, problems, and conditions with which the government body dealt. This information would be useful for various kinds of research. Schellenberg also described some of the criteria and techniques employed by federal archivists when judging evidential and informational value. To judge the evidential value of records, an archivist should know, in general terms: (1) the position of each office in the administrative hierarchy of an agency; (2) the functions performed by each office; and (3) the activities carried on by each office in executing a given function.[20] When determining evidential value, Schellenberg admonished, records should be evaluated in their entirety. The archivist should not make his evaluation on a piecemeal basis or on the basis of individual organizational units within an agency. When appraising the informational value of public records, on the other hand, the archivist need not be concerned with the source of the records, only with the information they contained. Such records could, therefore, be appraised piecemeal, at least in relation to other records produced by the agency. He did not contend that such appraisal should take place in a vacuum, however. Government records that contain information on a particular phenomenon should be appraised in relation to all other documentation on that phenomenon, regardless of its form, whether published or unpublished. That is when evaluating whether particular records deserve preservation on the basis of their informational value, the federal archivist should consider whether the same or similar information is available in other forms or places. The records universe is not limited to the physical records of the generating agency, but includes any source or agency that contains the data. For exampling, vital records are generated at the federal, state, and local level. They should, however, be kept only at the state and local level, Schellenberg asserted.

Although Schellenberg implied that fairly rigid criteria for evaluating the evidential value of federal records should be developed, he asserted that appraisal standards for informational value ought not be absolute; rather, they should be relative as to both time and place. Archivists should use different criteria in evaluating records of different periods. Furthermore, archivists in different archival institutions may use different criteria in evaluating similar types of records, because what is valuable to one institution may be valueless to another. Like Kahn, Schellenberg viewed consistency in judgment as neither possible nor desirable. He thought it better to spread the burden of documentation among many institutions, because one may preserve what another discards. Diverse judgments, Schellenberg wrote, "may well assure a more adequate social documentation."[21] Like his colleagues, he also recognized that statistical sampling and other special selection techniques were useful for reducing voluminous series, but he did not offer detailed instructions on how to conduct such selections.

International Efforts and Theories

Staff members of the National Archives of the United States were not alone in their struggle to develop principles and techniques that might provide an effective framework to guide archivists in their efforts to select from the vast record of the twentieth century that small percentage of documentation that society could afford to preserve permanently. As was noted earlier in this chapter, in his report to the Third International Congress of Archives, J.H. Collingridge reported that, in countries with established archival programs, the principles for selecting documents for preservation were, in broad outline, the same.[22] Generally preserved were papers having legal, administrative, historical, scientific, or cultural purposes. Generally destroyed were duplicates or copies, statistical primary materials, Hollerith cards, minor business papers, and printed matter. Policies on the retention of personal files varied from country to country, he found. Many countries reported that their biggest problems were how to keep up with the heavy flow of records and how best to appraise mixed classes of records—that is, groups in which records deserving preservation are interfiled with those that need not be preserved. Another problem cited was the handling of what the British call "particular instance" papers, such as vital records, census data, pension applications, and similar records that result from citizens' interactions with their government. Collingridge noted that the Grigg Committee, a committee appointed to study the Public Record Office's method of selecting records for preservation, had recommended that, except for birth, marriage, and death records, only those papers that are capable of being reduced to a statistical sample should be kept. Census data were included in this category. Collingridge also noted that the use of statistical sampling as a potential criterion for selection was not, despite the committee's recommendation, commonly viewed as feasible, inasmuch as archival organizations usually regard themselves as bound to keep papers likely to be useful for genealogical or biographical research. He added, however, the the Grigg Committee's view was supported by the report, *Paperwork Management*, presented to the U.S. Congress in 1955.[23]

The goals of economy and bureaucratic efficiency are not necessarily in harmony with the needs of research. As Collingridge was probably anticipating when he noted the unusual direction of the Grigg Committee's recommendation concerning sampling potential, scholars were not universally enthusiastic about the proposal. The issue of *Archivum* containing Collingridge's paper also included a response by Lisa Kaiser.[24] Kaiser argued for a more sophisticated approach to the selection of primary statistical materials. Using census records as an example, she asserted that the raw data in original completed questionnaires have tremendous value; research based on statistical samples of material that has itself been statistically sampled is suspect. Because researchers have increasingly focused on trends and structural changes in society and public life, preservation of all questionnaires of several successive censuses are needed, not selected examples of selected censuses. Kaiser called for the preservation of census data in particular, arguing that it constitutes the basic documentation of everyday life.

The Collingridge-Kaiser exchange points up the differing goals that archival appraisal seeks to satisfy. The evidential/informational dichotomy described by Schellenberg requires appraisers to attend to two different goals—the narrower one of documenting the history and operations of a particular agency, institution, or person, and the broader one of documenting a society and its people. As Schellenberg and others have noted, determination of evidential value is a more straightforward process. The operation of an agency can be adequately documented by correspondence files, financial records, policy manuals, and annual and project reports. Informational value, however, is more difficult to assess. As U.S. archivist Lewis J. Darter, Jr., observed, determination of informational value demands subjective judgments regarding importance, uniqueness, and usability of the records in question.[25] Not all archivists willingly accept the appropriateness of subjective judgment.

West German archivist Hans Booms is among those who strongly oppose reliance on subjective judgment in the appraisal process. In a paper presented at the Forty-Ninth German Archives Congress held in Dortmund in 1971, Booms sought to assess the adequacy of contemporary archival methodology for determining the content and form of the archival record that today's archivists will transmit to tomorrow's citizens.[26] Nothing the dramatic increase in record bulk, Booms asserted that only a small portion of that which is worthy of being preserved and transmitted can be transmitted. Archivists' recognition of the need to manage this bulk has had two consequences, according to Booms. First, archivists have changed the manner in which they acquire materials. Records management at the point of creation has become a commonly accepted notion. Second, though less generally accepted, is a change in methodological orientation of archivists. According to Booms, archivists have had to change from passive custodians of received materials to active determiners of record value. This new methodological orientation has caused archivists to adopt an active approach to appraisal. The theory of active appraisal is based on two assumptions. First, there is the assumption that the economic costs of custodianship are too high. Society simply cannot afford to retain most of the records that it produces. The second assumption is that the limitations on the amount of records that can be preserved become bearable when one recognizes the natural limitations of human powers and abilities to abstract. The problem of too much information is insurmountable, Booms argued. As long as technology cannot enable man to assimilate the mass of information available, his only course is to preserve less information.

The role change from passive custodian to active appraiser has important consequences for both archivists and the societies they serve. As the percentage of material that must be discarded increases, the role of the person charged with selection becomes proportionately greater. Furthermore, as that which is retained intact comes to represent an increasingly smaller portion of the preserved record and that which is treated, whether through thinning, sampling, or reorganization, comes to represent a larger portion, the preconceptions of the person processing the records becomes important. Booms asserted that the value system of the archivist's social and political environment, be it capitalist, socialist, or communist, becomes a fundamental determinant of what is preserved and transmitted. When using archival materials, therefore, the historian must recognize the environment in which the archivist was working, and the archivist is duty bound to objectify his principles of selection so they can be examined critically.

Earlier generations of archivists lacked objective selection criteria, Booms contended, because they were concerned in a speculative way with the records' future value. Booms opposed this speculative approach, arguing instead for an objective evaluation method that flows from the value system of the information universe that the archivist is responsible for transmitting. He rejected the possibility of proceeding in a deductive fashion from a given theoretical view of society—an approach advocated by archivists in some socialist countries. The proper approach, according to Booms, is to analyze, in an inductive fashion, smaller, more manageable social structures. This approach will give archivists an appropriate methodology for ascertaining which materials are suitable for preservation and transmittal. The purpose of this preservation and transmission can be, in the pluralistic structure of modern industrial society, a rationally structured total social documentation of public life in all its varieties.

Booms noted that this methodology assumes that the evaluation of what will be transmitted will proceed in a total social environment, requiring that archivists no longer make their evaluations solely on the basis of, or only within, their own archival environment. It requires that they discover a way to cooperate and to coordinate their work beyond the differences in levels of responsibility and areas of documentation. He acknowledged that, because the problems of dealing with bulk are so great, the archivist must frequently confer with scholars from other fields. The role of these colleagues, however, is to advise archivists in regard to materials they have already acquired. Only archivists can determine what materials should be preserved; the responsibility cannot be delegated. According to Booms, by following the new methodology, archivists will not speculate on what future historians may want, but will create a record that reflects today's values. The archivist's job, he asserted, is to document society in all its multiplicity and to transmit to posterity a manageable amount of records.

The most extensive discussion of archival appraisal is provided by Swedish archivist Nils Nilsson in his textbook, *Arkivkunskap*.[27] Described by his colleague Åke Kromnow as Sweden's foremost expert on the appraisal and destruction of public records, Nilsson recognizes the serious organizational and financial problems that modern records pose. He sets out, therefore, in good textbook fashion, the theoretical and practical considerations he believes form the basis of sound appraisal.

Nilsson's primary focus is on appraisal of records of government, industry, and associations. Assessment of documents whose content is unique are affected by different considerations, which he discusses separately. In regard to appraisal of governmental and organizational records, Nilsson lists five criteria or factors that he contends form the basis for weeding decisions: (1) reliability; (2) completeness; (3) comparability; (4) cost of preservation; and (5) density. He asks, is the information in the documents reliable enough to form the basis for conclusions of some durability? Is it complete enough that it is usable for research into generalized phenomena? He notes that, when a record group or series covers only a small area or has been strongly decimated through losses, the reasons favoring destruction gain in strength. Comparability refers both to the availability of similar materials and the structure of the records being appraised. Is the structure of the series such that comparisons with similar material from other points in time can be made? The greater the potential for comparison, the more likely the records should be preserved. Can the documents be preserved for a long period of time without costly reduction or transfer to another medium? If the answer is no, they are likely candidates for destruction. Finally, is the density of valuable information high enough to warrant retention? Preservation of a voluminous collection in which the information of interest exists only in low density can incur costs that are not defensible, Nilsson asserts. He acknowledges, however, that new technologies may make it economical to retain less information-dense materials than in the past.

Record content often determines the extent and the form of weeding, Nilsson notes. In particular, records that reflect individual variations of general or well-known themes, such as documents concerning the vacations of civil servants or the purchasing of supplies, are frequently subject to extensive weeding. The general principles and practices documented in such records are also evidenced in rules and regulations, precedents, established cases, and related appeals processes. Because the application of the rules in individual cases is of little interest and because such series are often very bulky, they are primary candidates for weeding. The archivist is justified in saving the individual cases in such series only when (1) the requirements of research cannot be satisfied by related materials or through some sort of selection process; (2) coverage in related materials is incomplete; or (3) total weeding might adversely affect a network of references that holds the archives together. Nilsson adds that one approach to reducing this type of record group is to preserve what he calls typical or prototype examples, which will, in the future, provide a picture of what was eliminated, create the opportunity for a reconstruction of the flow of work in a particular department, and show which material formed the basis for the related materials or summaries that were preserved. He describes several methods for deriving the prototype examples.

Contending that weeding is defensible only if it can be brought about at a reasonable cost, Nilsson argues for series-level weeding in most instances. Because weeding at the document level is difficult, expensive, and time consuming, it can be justified only in special cases, such as if the documents are easy to recognize, if the saving of space is considerable, or if individual documents (for example, letters or drawings) may warrant special handling anyway.

Having presented the principles on which any records-reduction program should be based, Nilsson describes methods for implementing such a program. Because he focuses primarily on series-level weeding, he includes an extensive overview of the principles and methods of statistical sampling. While some of the sampling applications Nilsson describes may be more feasible in countries such as Sweden than in larger, more administratively fragmented nations such as the United States, most of his recommendations will be at least partially transferable. His description of records management at the point of creation, or what he calls weeding at the source, is also informative, perhaps because it is based on long experience. Nilsson contends that this form of weeding has been applied longer and more consistently in Sweden than in any other country.

Like Booms, Nilsson advocates weeding in coordination with other archival institutions, but warns of the need for carefully planned programs and adequate safeguards. He also urges archivists to consult with experts from many fields and especially with the administrator of the department that generated the records being processed, because the administrator's knowledge of the activity documented and the means of retrieving information from the records form an obvious point of origin for the appraisal. Nilsson emphasizes, however, the weeding cannot be seen only from the point of view of the archives' generator. The importance that the documents may have for other activities, for judicial guarantees of due process, and for research must also be considered. In addition, the weeding methods at agencies having comparable documents must be ascertained before the archivist can determine to what extent the weeding should be carried.

Both Nilsson and Booms advise archivists to seek advice from scholars and administrators. Both also warn their colleagues that the final decision-making responsibility lies with the archivist, not the consultant. The two men differ, however, with regard to the assumptions upon which they are basing their advice. While Booms urges archivists to resist speculation about the future value of records and focus exclusively on accurately representing the function and value of the documents within the environment in which they were generated, Nilsson adheres to the more traditional view that archivists should consider future research needs when making appraisal decisions. Nilsson recognizes the difficulties inherent in the latter approach. Noting that, over time, new branches of science are created and new methods and questions emerge in established ones, he informs his readers that one has to learn to operate with significant margins of uncertainty.

Although Nilsson describes appraisal principles that were derived primarily from his work with government records, he contends that many of the principles are applicable to the evaluation of nongovernmental records, particularly those produced by businesses, institutions, and organizations. He urges custodians of these records to develop weeding plans that (1) describe the types of documents to be weeded and (2) state when and how they are to be weeded. Nilsson believes that work on individual personal archives is not sufficiently developed to have generated general weeding principles. He notes, however, that the frequently unique character of personal archives suggests that archivists should be conservative in their weeding of such records.

An enthusiastic advocate of weeding, Nilsson likens the process to the forestry's practice of thinning out the woods, or what he calls cutting for light. Well-managed weeding can make important materials more readily available, but Nilsson warns that excessive or poorly planned weeding can result in the loss of information and can reduce the quality of the documentation that remains. Nilsson is also careful to remind his readers that weeding is only one solution to the problem of bulk. Improving the design of forms, writing on both sides of the paper, removing documents from half-filled ring binders and putting them in well-filled cartons, dense packing, and microfilming are among the other solutions he recommends. Weeding must be viewed as only one of several methods available to the custodians of modern records, Nilsson asserts.

No overview of records-appraisal literature should omit Michael Lutzker's thoughtful article, "Max Weber and the Analysis of Modern Bureaucratic Organizations: Notes Towards a Theory of Appraisal."[28] Recalling Frank Burke's lament that archivists lack a theoretical perspective, Lutzker urges his colleagues to draw upon the work of related disciplines, such as sociology, social psychology, and public administration, for the insights they provide about the nature of organizations and administrative processes. He contends that the work of organizational theoreticians such as Max Weber enables archivists to view records more perceptively and to understand the multitude of organizational, social, and environmental factors that shape the records. While one may be skeptical about Lutzker's speculations regarding the potential role of archivists within their own organizations, one can only applaud his primary assertion that, if archivists are to appraise records intelligently, they must understand the administrative processes that produce the records.

Directions for Future Research

As this review has demonstrated, the management of twentieth-century records is a complex and difficult task. Archivists the world over have sought to articulate some model or set of criteria that would guide them in their difficult task of determining which records, among the vast number produced each year, shall be preserved for transmission to posterity. To date, no single model or set of guidelines has emerged. The easiest way to handle such records would be to destroy them once they were no longer needed for the purposes for which they were generated. This is not an acceptable approach, however, both because civilized societies demand a record of their follies and accomplishments and because records have uses beyond those intended by their creators.

Archivists take seriously their responsibility to preserve for posterity a rich accumulation of usable documentation. They also recognize that society

can afford to preserve only a small proportion of those records that are potentially useful. The question they must answer, then, is, "What shall be
saved?"

The archival profession has come a long way in answering this question.
The literature of the 1930s and 1940s witnessed the first efforts of archivists
to articulate the special problem presented by large contemporary record
collections. In the succeeding years, as they gained experience and shared
ideas, archivists not only articulated the problems, they began to frame
solutions. New techniques such as disposition schedules, weeding at the
source, and statistical sampling were developed. The design of forms, filing
systems, and storage space became as much the concern of the archivist as of
the records manager; indeed the work of each increasingly overlapped.
Broader questions—concerning the role of archives in society and the
proper task of the archivist—were also examined. Archivists came to realize
that decisions regarding what shall be preserved and what shall be destroyed
are not made in a vacuum; they are shaped by often unrecognized social,
economic, and political factors.

The existing literature provides an important base on which the archival
profession can continue to build its theoretical and technical superstructure.
To date, much of the work, both in the United States and elsewhere, has
been carried out by government-employed archivists. This is only to be
expected. Government agencies such as the National Archives are better
funded and better staffed than most other archival institutions. Furthermore, the volume of materials they must handle means that they cannot
avoid confronting the particular problems presented by contemporary
records.

The work of the national archival agencies has served the broader
archival community well—and no doubt will continue to do so. More work is
needed, however. The literature of archives and records management is
scattered and fragmented—published primarily in the form of journal articles. The Society of American Archivists has begun to try to synthesize some
of this literature in its Basic Manual Series.[29] These booklets are not state-
of-the-art reviews for the experienced archivist, however; they are introduc-
tory texts for the beginning student. Nilsson's volume was also written as a
textbook, but the level of detail and sophistication makes it valuable to the
experienced professional as well as to the student. The publication of
a volume equal in quality to Nilsson's, or perhaps a full translation of the
Nilsson book, would be a beneficial step toward the development of a more
substantial literature.

Also needed are studies of the records of nongovernmental institutions,
disciplines, and discreet populations, such as specific racial groups or groups
of employees. Empirical research into the content, organization, and use of
different types of records will provide the hard information that archivists
need to fully understand the nature of their task and the means by which to

best accomplish it.[30] Case studies and interinstitutional studies of appraisal as carried out in particular institutions would also be useful, both to share practical knowledge with colleagues and to inform them of the extent and shape of existing documentation.[31] Which institutions are saving the records of independent farming, for example? What are they saving, and why? More important, perhaps, is what are they destroying, and why? What about machine-readable records? Archivists are just beginning to confront the special problems that these records present. Again, National Archives staff are taking the lead in examining these subjects, but studies in other institutional environments must follow.[32] The goal of such studies is not to reach a consensus, but to stimulate new ideas and develop greater understanding of the appraisal process. As in the past, some archivists will seek objective appraisal standards while other will continue to value what Nils Nilsson has called a strong belief in the experience-based judgment of the archivist.[33] Continuing divergence of opinion should not be viewed as troublesome, however. It is, as we have seen, both inevitable and useful—inevitable because archivists must carry out their work in widely varying political and institutional environments; useful because an ongoing dialogue serves to broaden the perceptions and enhance the understanding of archivists everywhere.

Notes

1. In this chapter, *appraisal* is used to mean, "The process of determining the value and thus the disposition of records based upon their current administrative, legal, and fiscal use; their evidential and informational or research value; their arrangement; and their relationship to other records." [Frank B. Evans, Donald F. Harrison, and Edwin A. Thompson, "A Basic Glossary for Archivists, Manuscript Curators, and Records Managers," *American Archivist* 37 (July 1974): 417.] It is not used in the sense of determining monetary value. The term *weed* is used in the sense of examining records "in order to remove permanently file units lacking continuing value." [Ibid., p. 431.]

2. Walter Whitehill, *Independent Historical Societies* (Boston: Boston Athenaeum, 1962), pp. 246–247.

3. W. Kaye Lamb, "The Fine Art of Destruction," in *Essays in Memory of Sir Hilary Jenkinson,* ed. Albert E.J. Hollaender for the Society of Archivists (Chichester: Moore and Tillyer, 1962), p. 50.

4. Donald R. McCoy, *The National Archives: America's Ministry of Documents, 1934-1968* (Chapel Hill: The University of North Carolina Press, 1978), p. 63.

5. J.H. Collingridge, "The Selection of Archives for Permanent Preservation," *Archivum* 6 (1956): 25; D.L. Evans introduces Mr. Collingridge's paper.

6. Åke Kromnow, "The Appraisal of Contemporary Records," *Archivum* 26 (1979):45–54. The complete text of this paper was published as *The Appraisal of Contemporary Records* (Washington, D.C.: General Services Administration, 1976). Mr. Kromnow's paper is the most comprehensive overview of appraisal practice and theory presently available.

7. "Report of the Ad Hoc Committee on Manuscripts Set Up by the American Historical Association in December 1948," *American Archivist* 14 (July 1951):232.

8. As noted in the preface, because a large portion of the existing literature focuses on appraisal of governmental records, the authors decided to limit this volume to nongovernmental records.

9. Philip C. Brooks. *What Records Shall We Preserve?*, Staff Information Paper 9, Reprint (Washington, D.C.: National Archives and Records Service, 1975), p. 6. Originally published in a slightly different form as "The Selection of Records for Preservation," *American Archivist* 3 (October 1940):221–234.

10. Ibid., p. 8.

11. Ibid., p. 9.

12. Philip C. Brooks, "Records Selection—A Cooperative Task," *Indian Archives* 7 (July-December 1953):79–86.

13. Brooks, "The Selection of Records," p. 234, footnote 7.

14. Emmett J. Leahy, "Reduction of Public Records," *American Archivist* 3 (January 1940):13–38.

15. G. Philip Bauer *The Appraisal of Current and Recent Records*, Staff Information Circulars, no. 13, June 1946, Reprint (Washington, D.C.: National Archives and Records Service, 1976).

16. Herman Kahn, "Mr. Kahn's Comments," in Bauer, *The Appraisal of Current and Recent Records*, p. 23.

17. Ibid.

18. Ibid.

19. Theodore R. Schellenberg, *Modern Archives: Principles and Techniques* (Chicago: University of Chicago Press, 1956). The chapter on appraisal standards was also published separately as *The Appraisal of Modern Public Records*, Bulletins of the National Archives, no. 8 (Washington, D.C.: National Archives and Records Service, 1956).

20. Ibid., p. 142.

21. Ibid., p. 149.

22. J.H. Collingridge, "The Selection of Archives," p. 32.

23. Commission on Organization of the Executive Branch of the Government, *Paperwork Management, Part I, in the United States Government, A Report to Congress* (Washington, D.C.: Government Printing Office, 1955).

24. Lisa Kaiser, "Selection of Statistical Primary Material," *Archivum* 6 (1956):75-80.

25. Lewis J. Darter, Jr., "Records Appraisal: A Demanding Task," *Indian Archives* 18 (January-June 1969):8.

26. Hans Booms, "Gesellschaftsordnung und Überlieferungsbildung: Probleme archivarischer Quellenbewertung," *Der Archivar* 25 (1972):pt. 1, cols. 23-28. For the full text of the author's paper, see "Gesellschaftsordnung: und Überlieferungsbildung: Zur Problematik archivarischer Quellenbewertung," *Archivalische Zeitschrift* 68 (1972).

27. Nils Nilsson, *Arkivkunskap* (Lund: Studentlitteratur, 1972), pp. 110–130.

28. Michael A. Lutzker, "Max Weber and the Analysis of Modern Bureaucratic Organization: Notes Toward a Theory of Appraisal," *American Archivist* 45 (Spring 1982):119-130; Frank G. Burke," The Future Course of Archival Theory in the United States," *American Archivist* 44 (Winter 1981):40-46.

29. See, for example, Maynard J. Brichford, *Archives & Manuscripts: Appraisal & Accessioning* (Chicago: Society of American Archivists, 1977). This was published in the Basic Manual Series.

30. An example of this type of research is a study of the documentation of the history of science currently underway at the Massachusetts Institute of Technology. The work is being sponsored jointly by the National Science Foundation and the Andrew W. Mellon Foundation. Its project director, Helen Slotkin, expects the results of the study to be forthcoming in 1985. The works of Patricia Aronsson and Philip Cronenwett, included as chapters 4 and 5, respectively, in this book, constitute additional examples.

31. See, for example, Chapter 2 of this book.

32. See, for example, Meyer Fishbein, "Appraising Information in Machine Language Form," *American Archivist* 35 (January 1972): 35-43; and Charles M. Dollar, "Appraising Machine-Readable Records," *American Archivist* 41 (October 1978): 423–430.

33. Nilsson, p. 68.

2

Records Management as an Appraisal Tool in College and University Archives

John Dojka and *Sheila Conneen*

The decade from 1962 to 1972 was a period of unparalleled upheaval and growth for U.S. institutions of higher learning. Points of view differ on the actual nature of this period, ranging from "the disintegration and collapse of higher education as we knew it" to "one of the most creative and fertile transitional periods in the history of western education" schools of thought. The only point of agreement is that it was indeed a remarkable period, the effects of which will continue to influence the fundamental character and direction of academia for years to come.

The forces at work in this period were complex and interrelated. They included extraordinarily high levels of federal, state, and local funding; the coming of age of the postwar baby-boom generation; the questioning of the relevance of curriculum and the authorities who determined it; the belief in the university as a primary agent of social change; open-enrollment admissions policies; the extension of opportunities for higher education to formerly excluded minority groups; and the assumption that a college degree was a requisite for employment, even in fields formerly considered within the purview of technical education.

As a result, the contemporary college or university archives must now be able to document the activities of an institution that is simultaneously a community of scholars, an amorphous sociopolitical organization, and a subculture replete with its own peculiar values and rituals. This diversity has forced archivists to reexamine their appraisal criteria and techniques.

The challenge of reformulating and broadening appraisal criteria to meet these changing perceptions of institutions of higher learning has been complicated by a chronologically parallel phenomenon, the information explosion of the 1960s and 1970s. The net result is a radical increase in the scale of the appraisal problems confronting college and university archivists. Although the problems of intellectual and physical control posed by the rising volume of documentation have reached crisis proportions in the past ten years, generally there has not been a corresponding increase in program budgets and staffing to enable archivists to respond effectively to the crisis. Most college and university archives are still one- or two-person shops with very modest resources.

With smaller institutions annually churning out thousands of feet of paperwork and larger institutions surpassing the ten-thousand-foot mark, the task of appraisal—identifying and segregating the relatively small percentage of records worthy of permanent preservation—has become a critically significant, yet increasingly onerous, task. The alternative to responding vigorously and imaginatively to this challenge is to accept, by default, the degradation of the historical record of one's institution as stack areas fill up with thousands of feet of voluminous, repetitive records of little value to researchers.

Appraisal guidelines and checklists such a those provided by the Society of American Archivists' *Guidelines for College and University Archives*, although clearly important in helping to define the collecting universe, provide only a starting point for program development.[1] The underlying problem is not merely determining which records to collect, but also how to efficiently identify and segregate the 5 to 10 percent of permanently valuable records from the thousands of feet of paperwork produced in the course of a year's activity at even a modest-size institution. The archivist must now master the skills that will allow the intellectual and physical control of voluminous documentation.

The present problems of college and university archivists are analogous to those faced by the staff of the National Archives in the late 1930s and 1940s, when they were forced to develop procedures to cope with the mountains of paperwork produced by New Deal programs and the expansion of bureaucracy resulting from the country's entry into World War II. To fulfill their program mandates meaningfully, the archives staff had to shift from a passive custodial role to active intervention in the paperwork-producing cycle of the departments they were serving.[2] The National Archives facilitated this shift by developing a body of theory and procedure that shortly assumed a life and purpose of its own: records management.

The concept of applying these same records-management techniques to college and university records is, of course, not new. By the mid-1960s, several large universities had undertaken ambitious, full-scale records programs, modeled on the procedures developed at the National Archives and refined by business corporations and state records-management programs.

Yet, despite the great amount of interest in records management in recent years, the expense, staffing, and space required for full-scale programs have proven prohibitively high for the majority of college and university archival programs. This does not mean, however, that the tools of records management must remain beyond the grasp of all but the most affluent institutions. Records management is emphatically not an all-or-nothing proposition. There is no reason why initial efforts at records management have to be full-scale, state-of-the-art programs right out of a textbook. There are choices to be made—some depending, it is true, on one's budget, but also depending to a great extent on one's imagination and initiative. The question should not be whether to establish a records program, but rather what size the program should be.

The purpose of this chapter is, therefore, to describe alternatives. By creative adaptation and use of records-management techniques, combined with the development of clearly articulated and stringently administered appraisal policies, the archivist can acquire tools proven effective in reducing the flood of contemporary documentation to manageable proportions and ensuring the quality of accessioned material. The solution presented here is feasible for college and university archives of all sizes because records-management programs do not necessarily have to be designed and implemented as full-scale programs that monitor the entire paperwork production of an institution. The latter portion of this chapter demonstrates how the Yale University Archives developed such a mid-level records-management program.

A flexible integration of records-management principles with archival practices and procedures can provide college and university archivists with the benefits of select records-management practices without intimidating costs. The broad spectrum of options ranges from an incremental approach that establishes a full-scale program over a number of years, expanding as resources and experience allow, to the simple integration of several records-management components into a repository's existing operation. Whatever strategy is chosen, archivists cannot afford to remain ignorant of records-management techniques.

To grasp the alternatives that are available, a basic understanding of three planning tools is needed: (1) a working definition of records-management theory and the objectives of a records program—in other words, a way of conceptualizing records management; (2) the components of basic program design; and (3) some guidelines for selecting program components.

Records Management: Defintion and Objectives

A foundation for the conceptualization of records management is the theory that the paperwork of an institution has a life cycle that is composed of distinct phases: records are created, used for some purpose, stored or filed for future reference, and eventually disposed of or deposited in archives for permanent retention (see figure 2–1).

Creation→ Active Use→ Inactive Use→ Destruction/Archives Record

Figure 2–1. The Paperwork Life Cycle

In an institution where paperwork is managed effectively, there is an efficient, cost-effective flow of records through the phases of the paperwork life cycle. On the other hand, in an institution where paperwork is poorly managed, the flow of records through the life cycle is retarded, chaotic, or nonexistent. Records and the information they contain are difficult to retrieve, and costly duplication of paperwork is a frequent occurrence. The net effect of poor management is a decrease in the efficiency of the institution and an inflation of its operating costs. It also makes archival functions, particularly appraisal, extremely difficult and time consuming to perform.

The basic purpose, therefore, of a records-management program is to monitor records, regardless of type, to ensure that they do indeed pass efficiently and at minimum cost through the creation, use, inactive storage, and disposal or permanent-retention phases.

Records managers translate this general objective into four basic goals for institutional records programs:

1. To assure the maintenance, protection, retention, and disposition of records in accordance with an institution's operational, legal, tax, and historical requirements.
2. To avoid costly use of office space and the need to purchase filing equipment and other related equipment.
3. To reduce time spent filing and retrieving records and to make the records more readily accessible.
4. To ensure that records that have outlived their usefulness are destroyed.

Archivists are necessarily concerned with these four traditional goals of records managers because current records-maintenance practices directly determine the quality of an institution's archives in terms of the completeness, integrity, and accessibility of the historical record. Archivists' unique position in respect to the records of an institution allows them to become the catalytic agent in rationalizing the production and flow of records within that institution, thereby saving substantial sums in both direct and indirect expenditures, as well as increasing the institution's administrative efficiency.

Selectively adopting records-management elements into an archival program, even a limited rather than a full-scale program, enables archivists to do their jobs more thoroughly, more effectively, and, in the long run, at a lower cost. These gains are achieved by implementing various combinations of the program elements or components:

1. Records-retention and disposition scheduling.
2. Design and management of files.
3. Clerical personnel workshops and procedural manuals.
4. Records-center operations.

5. Microfilm service.
6. Vital-records security.
7. Forms design and management.
8. Reprographics control.
9. Word-processing management.
10. Source-data automation.
11. Mail and correspondence management.
12. Machine-readable records management.

Each of these program elements is a technique or procedure designed to monitor a specific phase of the paperwork life cycle. For example, forms reports, and correspondence management affect the creation phase of records; files design and management cover the period when the records are actively used and must be retrieved quickly; records-center management treats the period of inactivity, when records are most efficiently housed in low-cost storage facilities; and records-control scheduling informs office staffs when they may dispose of or transfer to the archives various types of records (see figure 2–2).

The concept of a paperwork life cycle provides the archivist with an analytical framework for breaking the records production, handling, and storage activities of an academic institution into their component parts in order to isolate problems and implement effective solutions.

Elements of Basic Program Design

Existing college and university records programs usually can be grouped into one of three categories according to size. In the first category are large-scale programs, frequently serving multicampus systems, which generally operate independently of an archival program reporting directly to the institution's chief fiscal or academic officer. These programs typically employ a number of records managers and a variety of technical specialists. In the second category are midlevel programs, which are commonly administered by an archivist who has a records officer, a records center, and,

Creation	Active Use	Inactive Use	Destruction Archives
Forms design	Files design	Records-center	Records schedules
Reprographics	Workshops,	management	Records-center
control	manuals development	Microfilm	management
Correspondence	Records	service	
management	schedules	Records	
Word processing		schedules	
Source-data			
automation			

Figure 2–2. Program Components Designed to Monitor Phases of the Record Life Cycle

perhaps a microfilm operation. The third category consists of the many programs administered by archivists and special-collections librarians who devote a fifth to a quarter of their time to records programs and have absolutely no hope of ever hiring a full-time records officer or establishing a records center.

Therefore, the general scale of the prospective program is the first major element to be determined. Deciding on the size may not be within the archivist's power; it may be a fait accompli—already determined by administrators of the institution. Despite the archivist's best efforts to marshal evidence on the potential benefits of a records program, the administration simply may be unwilling to commit substantial resources to a new program. If this is the case, and it is quite likely to be, there are alternatives available to the archivist.

The archivist should focus on what can be accomplished with the existing time and resources, not on what could be done if only x amount of dollars were available. The important point to bear in mind is that the size or scale of a program does not necessarily have anything to do with its quality or effectiveness. Bigger, given the fiscal constraints within which most college and university archivists operate, is not necessarily better. There are highly effective, state-of-the-art programs in each of the three size categories.

No matter what their size, all programs share the same basic definition of records management and the same goals noted earlier; where they differ is in the number and type of specific program components they incorporate. For example, a large-scale, well-funded program might conceivably engage in all or most of the program components, including the more technical and expensive elements such as source-data automation and word processing. Such a program might monitor every phase in the record life cycle from creation to disposition.

A midlevel program might consist of a half-dozen components, such as a records center, centralized microfilming service, or an institutionwide records survey. A small, part-time operation might well concentrate its activities in two or three low-technology, maximum-impact components, such as records-control scheduling, files management, clerical training sessions, and procedural manuals. What every archivist should remember is that viewing records management as a series of program components directed at monitoring specific phases of the record life cycle gives him the flexibility to tailor a program to the institution's own needs, achieving maximum impact while expending the fewest resources.

If both resources and support are available, the archivist should by all means design a program that links together components to monitor the complete records life cycle. If, on the other hand, the only resource available is the archivist's own time, frequently the equivalent of one workday a week, the program should consist of one or two maximum-impact components. It is possible to run a very effective, albeit small, program without hiring a full-time records officer, without establishing a records center, without undertaking an exhaustive survey of the institution's paperwork, and even without having a formally recognized program.

Factors Determining Choice of Program Components

Three factors will help to determine the choice of program components. They are: (1) the size of the proposed program; (2) the scale of the paperwork problem; and (3) the nature of the institution's archives program. First, the projected size of the program must be balanced against the relative expense and impact of the program components. As noted earlier, some of the components, such as source-data automation and word processing, are highly technical and apply to a relatively narrow spectrum of the paperwork life cycle. The cost of these components will tend to limit their use to larger records programs. It is also conceivable that some records-management activities are already being performed by other units in the institution and that even a modest-size records program could establish links and coordinate its activities with the units responsible for automation projects.

Components such as a records center, a centralized microfilming service, or an institutionwide records survey will be within the realm of possibility for midlevel programs. Other low-technology components, particularly records-control scheduling, files management, clerical staff training sessions, and the development of procedural manuals, will have a broad impact on the records of an institution with a relatively small input of time and money. The basics of these components are generally familiar to archivists or are relatively easily learned (see figure 2–3).

A second factor to be considered when choosing program components is the scale of the institution's paperwork problems. Assessment of paperwork problems can be done in several ways, depending on available resources. An initial institutionwide survey will enable the archivist to gather literally years' worth of planning data and problem-solving ideas, but, because of the cost and time involved, it is out of the reach of many archivists. Because of the nature of archivists' work, however, many already have a great deal of insight into the paperwork problems of their institutions. This knowledge, perhaps polished and formalized a bit, should be enough to facilitate intelligent planning.

Paperwork problems are endemic to institutions. For each type of problem that an archivist encounters, there is a corresponding program

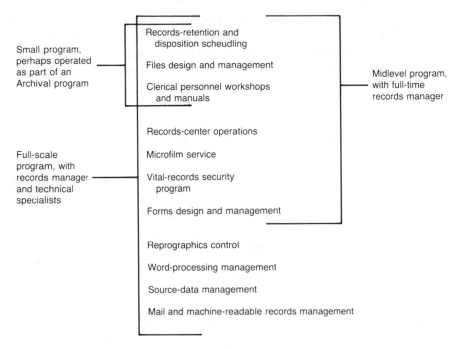

Small program,
perhaps operated
as part of an
Archival program

Records-retention and
  disposition scheudling

Files design and management

Clerical personnel workshops
  and manuals

Midlevel program,
with full-time
records manager

Full-scale
program, with
records manager
and technical
specialists

Records-center operations

Microfilm service

Vital-records security
  program

Forms design and management

Reprographics control

Word-processing management

Source-data management

Mail and machine-readable records management

Figure 2–3. Choice of Program Components for Different-Size Programs

component to correct or at least control it. Five of the most typical problems
are:

1. Backlogs of outdated records, which cause overcrowded and ineffi-
cient use of office and storage areas—the paperjammed offices, attics, and
basements familiar to most archivists. Solutions to this problem include
records-control scheduling to authorize the disposal of records after they
have served their purpose; development of efficient, low-cost storage areas
by establishing a records center or upgrading the existing storage areas in
university offices into a number of mini-records centers serviced by the staff
who use them; and, possibly, microfilming.

2. Poorly planned and serviced filing systems, which promote ineffi-
cient storage and retrieval of information. Most archivists recognize such
filing systems at a glance; they are the ones that are nightmares to appraise
and weed. Potential solutions include files design and management, which is
very similar to the classing of records in series that one does when processing
archival material; training sessions and manuals on filing procedures for
clerical staff members; and automation of records that contain large quantities of standardized paperwork.

3. Inadequate security for vital fiscal, legal, and personnel records,
including student transcripts. These records are the institutional equivalent
of the documents that a prudent homeowner would keep in a safe-deposit

box; their loss or destruction would be a disaster of major proportions. A likely solution to this problem is a vital records-security microfilm program involving off-site storage of a film copy of the records.

4. Duplication, unneeded, and outmoded records, forms, correspondence, memoranda, and reports. A variety of procedures, including forms and correspondence management and source-data automation, can control such paperwork proliferation.

5. Poorly designed forms and office procedures, which cause paperwork snarls and inefficiencies. These can be corrected by forms-design and forms-control programs, reprography control, and general paperwork-procedure analysis.

The third factor that will determine the choice of program components is the nature of the institution's archival program. Given the huge quantities of documentation produced by even the smallest educational institutions, the task of identifying, appraising, and preserving the 5 to 10 percent of permanently valuable records is becoming increasingly burdensome. Selectively adapting records-management elements into an archival program, even if not a full-scale effort, will enable the archivist to perform more thoroughly, more efficiently, and, in the long run, at lower cost. When picking program components, the archivist should choose those elements that clearly justify their value in terms of the individual archival program. That is, the components chosen should simplify or save time on some archival procedure already being performed, such as appraisal, processing, or description.

As noted earlier, the size of the records-management program, scale of paperwork problems, and nature of the institution's archives program will determine how the program components rank. There are three components—records-retention and disposition scheduling; files design; clerical training sessions and development of manuals—that should, in most cases, be the core elements of a program, regardless of its size. These components are relatively inexpensive to implement; they will have a maximum impact on the records of an institution; and they will have a direct relationship to many of the tasks performed by an archival program.

Essentially, retention and disposition schedules are checklists that inform offices of how long they must retain various types of records and when they may discard or transfer records to inactive storage or to the archives. The establishment of retention and disposition schedules is a relatively routine procedure, but it is the single most effective way to remove records systematically from offices. Scheduling can facilitate the eventual destruction of a very high percentage of an institution's paperwork. Even if this component were the sole activity of a records program, its accomplishment would be significant because it gets paper out of the system. By establishing retention and disposition schedules, the archivist is, in effect, performing archival appraisal on a large portion of the institution's records before they reach the archives.

Second priority should be given to files design and management. The purpose of this component is to encourage the adoption of uniform records-keeping systems. Just as records are arranged into a series during processing, like material is filed together in order to facilitate description and retrieval. Office personnel benefit because records in a well-designed filing system are easier to service and retrieve. The records officer or archivist benefits because files can be appraised and weeded according to disposition schedules at what is, in effect, series level as opposed to folder or document level. Thus, files design and management is a cognate of retention and disposition scheduling. If files are to be purged expeditiously from large filing systems, materials of a given type, such as budget, personnel, and general correspondence files, should be filed together. Each will have a different retention period. If filed as distinct series, removal of one type from the file is a very simple task. From the archivist's point of view, files design can have a high payoff because it simplifies appraisal, file weeding, and processing. It is also a key factor in avoiding the labor-intensive preparation work that must otherwise precede most microfilm projects.

The third core element of any program should be training sessions and the development of procedures manuals on basic records storage and retrieval techniques. Most colleges and universities employ hundreds of clerical personnel who bear the primary responsibility for the day-to-day maintenance of the institution's records. To a great extent, the activities of the whole institution depend upon the efficient and reliable functioning of the clerical staff. Yet most institutions invest little effort to ensure that clerical staff members are given adequate training and assistance in carrying out the basic record-keeping duties that make up a large part of their work. Workshops and manuals are efficient media for reaching large numbers of these employees. Their purpose is twofold—to acquaint clerical and administrative staff with basic records-storage and records-retrieval techniques, especially files design, and to build grass-roots support among people whose cooperation is vital to the success of a records program. The wise archivist will take every opportunity to involve the institution's clerical staff in the records program.

If the resources exist to support them, the next components the archivist should choose are a records center and a centralized microfilming service. A forms-design and forms-control program should follow. Other components should be added as time and circumstances allow.

Programs operating on a shoestring budget should explore alternatives to a records center and filming service. One option for temporary storage of inactive records is to upgrade existing basement or attic storage areas to create a series of mini-records centers, which would be serviced by the staff who use them. While this alternative is by no means ideal, it is the sort of compromise that can work effectively. As an alternative to providing microfilm services, the archives can act as an institutionwide clearinghouse for information on filming. The archivist can advise offices as to when filming is appropriate, participate in the design of film-conversion projects, and make referrals to reputable microfilm vendors.

Another option for small programs, especially for archivists who may want to incorporate several records components into their archival program as opposed to establishing a separate records-management program, is to employ a project-oriented strategy. Most of the program components, with the exception of general records-retention and disposition scheduling, do not necessarily have to be applied to all of the units in an institution at the same time. The project approach would involve the use of records-management techniques, such as files design, to correct problems in a unit that, from an archival point of view, is a problem child—a unit whose records are particularly difficult to appraise, weed, and process. Using this approach, the archivist could, over time, gradually move through the institution unit by unit, concentrating on areas with the most serious problems.

Another approach for a small or part-time program would be to implement two or three components in stages over a period of months or years. For example, the archivist could, during the first year, use any available resources to establish retention and disposition schedules; the next year, he could fund file-design workshops.

Whatever the scope of the endeavor—whether full-scale or part-time—the archivist can be sure that any efforts invested in records management will more than repay themselves in terms of benefits to the institution and its archival program.

An Example of a University
Records-Management Program

Our experience in implementing a joint archival records-management program at Yale University illustrates a number of the recommendations described in the preceding sections. The Yale University Archives undertook a records-management project because, despite its long history and prominence among colleges and universities, Yale University had made no sustained, systematic effort to retain its records before 1978. As a result, much of the documentation of the university's history, especially the records of the professional schools, department files, and faculty papers, had been relegated to basements and attics, where they were subject to water, insect, and fire damage or outright destruction during periodic "house cleanings." Over the years, a sizable quantity of records made its way into the archives and was rescued from imminent destruction by a small staff, working under pressure and often without the benefit of archival training. As a result, much of the accessioned material was poorly appraised and received only cursory processing and description. What occurred was a series of holding actions rather than the beginning of a systematic records-management program.

That the university's records had great research value was shown by the archives' research statistics. By the mid-1970s, approximately 150 scholars had conducted research using university records each year; 2,000 requests for files had been received from administrative offices; and there had been over 500 written or telephone request for information that could only be found by research in university records. There was no reason to believe that the quantities of records mouldering in university attics and basements or those to be produced in future years would be any less valuable than those already in the archives. An important resource was and would continue to be unavailable to administrators and researchers.

It was clear to the archives staff that practices that had been barely adequate in the past could not deal with problems posed by contemporary documentation. Like all archival repositories, Yale's archives suffered from the traditional problems of inadequate space, staff, and budget. In addition, the staff was encountering what were, to us, new problems. We noted a staggering increase in the university's production of paperwork and a growing number of requests from offices for assistance with records storage and retrieval. We realized that both current holdings and future accessions would have to be assessed in light of their quality as historical evidence if we were to justify the effort required to maintain and describe them adequately.

We had long suspected that the nature and quantity of the university's paperwork had changed dramatically as a result of office automation, particularly high-speed photocopying, word processing, and electronic data processing. University offices and storage areas housed 35,000 linear feet of records, which were increasing at a rate of 10,000 linear feet each year. Since 1960, the university's record production had trebled. This increase had paralleled the development and proliferation of photocopying equipment and other automated office procedures. The increase from both internal and external sources of duplicated reports, memoranda, committee minutes, and correspondence copies was largely responsible for the increased volume of paper that office staff had to manage. Coping with the increased rate of paper flow was placing unbearable demands on the archives' resources. If we were to continue to fulfill our program's mandate, we would have to devise more effective means of dealing with the complex problems posed by contemporary documentation, particularly the problems of volume and appraisal (see appendix 2A).

The Records Survey

During the fiscal year 1975–76, the archives staff, with the strong support of the university librarian, began a systematic campaign to improve services offered. Once the archives had acquired a storage area with proper fire protection, freight access, lighting, and shelving for 16,000 cubic feet of records, the staff's next objective was to gain support for a universitywide records survey. We saw the survey as multifaceted—a means to reexamine both our internal procedures and our role within the university, as well as to encourage assessment of the historical documentation contained in the university's records.

The survey had five major goals:

1. To determine the type, location, quantity, and condition of records currently in university offices and storage areas.
2. To assess the university's paperwork problems in order to develop recommendations to the university administration for a records-management program that would make maximum use of existing facilities.
3. To accession university records of permanent historical and administrative value.
4. To gather planning data for reorganizing and updating the university's archival program, including the systematization of internal controls, such as appraisal and accessioning procedures and the determination of processing, preservation, and description priorities.
5. To gain support and understanding throughout the university community of the value of a well-organized and funded archival program.

Speed and additional staffing were crucial. Covering Yale's huge physical plant and over five hundred administrative offices would have taken a single person three to four years. Were this possible, by the time the survey was completed, much of the support engendered in the university offices would have withered for lack of follow-up.

A more serious reason for urging speed was the university's financial position. Since the late 1970s, Yale, like most universities, had suffered severely from inflation. These financial constraints posed both threats and potential benefits for the future of the archival program. It was clear that, if the archives did not act quickly, administrative belt-tightening measures would cause marginal storage areas to be used for office expansion in lieu of building new facilities; this would mean the wholesale destruction of records housed there. However, if the archives seized the initiative, it had an opportunity to demonstrate to an increasingly cost-conscious administration the potential savings of a combined archival/records-management program.

With joint funding from the National Historical Publications and Records Commission and the Yale University provost, secretary, and librarian, we performed an eighteen-month universitywide records survey, using one professional and two clerical-technical staff members. The components were:

1. Planning phase (one month).
2. Universitywide records survey (twelve months).
3. Internal survey of archives holdings and redesign and implementation of an archival/records-management program using data collected in surveys (six months).
4. Dissemination of information through a report and workshop.

Perhaps the single most important aspect of the planning phase was the design and testing of the multipurpose survey instrument—the form on which data for each file series of the university's records were to be recorded. The design of our survey form was based on a review of sample forms from thirty federal, corporate, and university programs; the body of professional literature regarding surveying and records management; and the information needed for planning and updating the archival/records-management program at Yale.

After the survey form was designed, it was tested, along with the interviewing techniques of the survey staff, in a pilot survey of the records of the School of Nursing and the University Library. (See appendix 2B for examples of the survey forms.) Using these forms, we surveyed over 35,000 linear feet of records in more than 500 offices and administrative units and conducted over 600 interviews with deans, department heads, administrative assistants, and secretaries in our year-long survey.

Typical Record-Keeping Problems

During the survey, we identified several offices that had problems typical of many of the university offices. We then devised solutions for these offices' problems, illustrating the benefits of a records-management program. Using these offices as examples, we promoted our program to the university administration. As our examples demonstrated, the benefits obtainable from a records-management program are:

1. The rewards of attention to current files maintenance, both for the office concerned and for the archivist.
2. The upgrading of an existing storage area to allow more efficient use of the area.
3. The removal of inactive records, freeing valuable space.

The record-keeping problems of the president's office were typical of many university offices. Office files were maintained in a centralized alphabetical system extending over a dozen four-drawer filing cabinets. For staff members, retrieving information from the files was an uncertain undertaking and the source of frequent frustration and complaints. Information on a single topic was frequently filed under a half-dozen or more headings, such as proper names, committee, subject, or university office. Consequently, much of the information on a given topic was frequently lost because the staff did not know under which heading it might be filed.

To compound the problem, there was no procedure for periodically weeding the files. When drawers became overcrowded, another cabinet was added and the whole system enlarged, a time-consuming yearly ritual. Individual files were frequently undated so, when the staff did attempt to discard material, they had to search the contents to each file folder, document by document, to determine dates.

Working with university archives staff, the president's office staff redesigned the filing system using a classed scheme that broke the massive alphabetical system into smaller, more manageable units according to broad subject area, function, and the hierarchy of the university, thus narrowing the area to be searched for any given records. Within each unit of the system, files were systematically dated and color coded to allow staff members to quickly identify and dispose of outdated information, ending the need to periodically expand the entire system by adding new cabinets.

Most important, a file index was established to act as an authority list on filing decisions and to facilitate cross-references between subjects. This procedure effectively solved the problem of information's being filed and forgotten under a number of different headings.

The changes in this system were made gradually, as time allowed and without disrupting office procedures, and a higher priority was assigned to the task of maintaining retrievable records. The result is a filing scheme that is one of the most efficient on campus. Staff working with the records can quickly file and retrieve information; outdated records are efficiently segregated for disposal; and the system can be learned quickly by new staff members.

From the archives' point of view, the benefits of this system are that files can be readily appraised by the classed units (which are essentially series); finding aids are prepared by office staff before the records are transferred; and the office has a new consciousness of the value of keeping in close touch with the archives staff. The time saved on appraisal, processing, and preparation of finding aids made the investment well worth the initial time spent in setting up the system.

In a dean's office, we showed how to make better use of existing storage areas through the utilization of records-management techniques. Over the years, a vault had become jammed with records, some of them dating from the turn of the century. The records were inaccessible, dirty, and extremely difficult for the staff to service. The backlog of semiactive records that should have been moved into the storage area was piling up in the offices, taking up space and making records currently in use difficult to retrieve. To coordinate the organization of the storage vault, we removed significant documentation to the archives, discarded appropriate material, and reorganized filing equipment. As a result, ineffectively used space was transformed into an efficient file room capable of receiving records from prime office areas as they become semiactive. Yearly visits by archives staff ensure a continued flow of historically valuable records to the archives and of worthless records to the incinerator.

Next, our work in coordination with a staff member from the office of the vice-president for finance and administration resulted in the removal of such a large quantity of records that space was created for two offices. Several-hundred feet of records in a top-floor storage area were destroyed after screening, and the remainder were consolidated more efficiently. In addition, eighty linear feet of semiactive records dating from the 1930s to the 1970s were removed from the file room. The records proved to be an important source for documenting the university's development and were accessioned into archives. We now provide reference service to the office whenever information is needed from the records and continue to accession other records as they become semiactive. The filing room from which we removed the records was subsequently turned into an office.

Internal Survey of the University Archives

In addition to the universitywide survey, we also performed an internal survey of the holdings of the archives. As noted earlier, despite the lack of a systematic archival program, nearly 10,000 linear feet of university records had made their way into the library by 1979. Although valuable, many of the records were in poor physical condition and lacked all but the most preliminary processing and finding aids. Since one of the purposes of the grant was to gather data to update and reorganize the archival program, it was necessary to review accessioned records to (1) assess needed work and (2) arrive at a realistic work plan for accomplishing the task. To gather the data, team members undertook a four-week survey, including shelf reading, of all records in the archives. The type of information gathered for each accession included: location in stacks, office of origin, quantity, description (both form and broad subject), physical condition, processing needs, and recommendations on work to be performed. (See appendix 2C for the internal survey form.)

Findings of the Records Survey

At the conclusion of the eighteen-month study period, we analyzed the data we had gathered from both the campuswide survey and the internal survey of the archives. We determined that poor record-handling and maintenance procedures represented substantial costs to the university. Unlike energy waste, mismanagement of recorded information was increasing operating expenses in ways not readily measurable or apparent to administrators. The costs were insidious, unlikely to appear directly as expenditure in accounting statements. They emerged indirectly in the form of inefficiently used office space and equipment; routine procedures snarled in tangles of paperwork; inability to retrieve needed information quickly; and intangibles such as the poor morale of staff members who had to cope with the day-to-day headaches resulting from mismanaged records. The tendency within the university had been to accept such conditions and their accompanying expense and frustration as part of the normal working environment. As a result, there was neither a coherent policy for identifying and saving those records that had continuing administrative value nor a procedure for disposing of those records that did not.

The specific problems identified by the survey fell into seven categories:

1. Use of office and storage space.
2. Disposition of records.
3. Information retrieval and storage.
4. Automation.
5. Use of microforms.
6. Security of vital records.
7. Instruction and information on records-management policies and procedures.

Records Management as a Solution

Through the use of the elements of records management, we were able to address the problems identified by the survey. The findings of our survey and the results of several pilot projects had convinced us of (1) the imperative need for a university records program and (2) the feasibility of establishing a midrange records-management program administered by the archives. Such a program would enable the staff to extend to the entire university services that had been performed in the past for a only few key administrative offices. Yet the program would require only minimal staff (one professional and one assistant at the clerical-technical level) and budget increases.

Therefore, we drafted a report that sought the support of the university administration for the establishment of a universitywide records program. We saw the report as essentially didactic, a short course for administrators on the problems of contemporary documentation and the applications of records-management principles.

Because we anticipated questions about the role automation could play in paperwork management, we attempted to address both its role in increasing the amount of paperwork produced in the university as well as its efficacy in offices whose principal function was record keeping. The familiarity we now had with the university offices and their records problems allowed us to explain the limited applicability of automated record-keeping procedures for the majority of offices.

The university's straitened finances made it tempting to emphasize the potential cost savings a records-management program could produce. However, we chose not to emphasize cost figures and statistics but to show instead specific examples of how a records-management program had worked successfully in the three representative offices described earlier. We did not want to lock ourselves into a position that would require us to justify our program each year in terms of cost savings; we stressed the increased efficiency and better utilization of existing facilities that would result from the program.

The report was presented to the president, the vice-president for finance and administration, the provost, and the secretary of Yale University in June 1980; funding for the program was authorized in August 1980.

Development of an Archival/Records-Management
Program

With the mandate provided by the administration, we began to tailor a program to fit the university's own needs rather than attempting to impose a rigid, standardized records-management program on the university's records. Using individual components also allowed us to commit ourselves only to program goals that we were fairly certain we could meet with the very limited resources available. We were leery of making any pie-in-the-sky promises to the administration.

We conceptualized our efforts as a joint archival/records-management program. Each records-management component had a direct linkage to an archival activity, and many of the links, such as records appraisal and disposition scheduling, were performed as the same function.

As archivists, approaching records management in this fashion provided us with the means of integrating records-management elements into our archival program, as opposed to developing a records-management program administered as a separate entity.

A significant step in our planning was to clarify our reasons as archivists for connecting ourselves with a records-management program. For us, this was a significant issue and proved to have a substantial impact on how we approached records management and how we designed our program. As noted, we wanted to establish clear linkages between the archival and records-management components of the program; the records-management elements would have to justify themselves by improving, facilitating, expediting, or reducing the expense of our archival responsibilities.

The reorganization of our archival program was to a large extent determined by the findings of the universitywide and internal surveys. From the results of those surveys, we were able to assess the weaknesses of the existing archival program and to formulate long-term solutions to the problems we had identified. Analysis of our data as well as the promising results of several pilot projects convinced us that the dilemmas posed by contemporary documentation were manageable if we focused attention on five areas:

1. Increasing input into the management of current records through the integration of elements of a records-management program into our archival program.
2. Rationalizing our processing procedures.
3. Making more extensive use of microforms.
4. Using tighter, more systematically applied appraisal standards.
5. Reappraising previously accessioned records.

Our guiding principles in planning a program that would focus on the five areas were:

1. To select program elements that specifically addressed problems identified by the survey.
2. To link together as many archival and records-management components as possible in order to avoid duplication within the program.
3. To make each records-management program element clearly justify its value in terms of the archival program—in order to be chosen, the element would have to simplify or save time on some archival procedure(s) already being performed, such as appraisal, processing, or description.
4. To design new program elements that would make maximum use of existing facilities and administrative structures.
5. To create a grass-roots program involving the staff in university offices to the maximum extent possible.

The reorganization of the archival component of the program was embodied in a series of program statements—core mission, collection policy, appraisal guidelines, and processing standards—drafted in conformity with the Society of American Archivists' college and university archives standards (see appendix 2D).

The reorganization specifically included the redesign of our internal control mechanisms, achieved by the institution of record groups, a new locator system, and a revised finding and filing system. We assigned a high priority to bringing all current holdings up to the minimum standards of physical control and description as described in appendix 2D.

Elements of the Records-Management Program

With our archival program in better order, we turned our attention to the design of the records-management component of our program. After reviewing data gathered during the survey, we decided to establish a records program that was midrange, a decentralized approach using a small staff to encourage and help offices to solve their own records problems. In this way, we felt we could work through and make the maximum use of existing staff and facilities.

The program elements we chose were those that we felt would have the greatest impact while using only the small staff we had available. There are nine major elements to our program, which are also implicit in the job description of the university archivist/records-management officer.

1. Establish records-retention and disposition schedules for dissemination to all university offices. The eventual destruction of 65 to 70 percent of all the university's records can be facilitated in this way. The model we followed was taken from the University of Missouri's records-management program.

Essentially, the schedule consists of a checklist indicating (a) which office is responsible for maintaining the official copy of the record in question and how long it should be maintained and (b) the location of unofficial copies, for example, in all university offices. The schedule also authorizes those units to discard the record after a specified period of time.

The establishment of retention and disposition schedules is a relatively routine procedure, but it is the single most effective way to systematically remove records from offices. In most of the university's offices, for example, the largest category of records is the general administrative subject-correspondence file. This category alone constitutes 20 percent of the total volume of university records. We scheduled these records to be held in offices no longer than five years and then to be destroyed after a review by the university archivist. Color coding or dating of folder tabs provide the office staff with an efficient means of identifying when the time limit for maintaining the records has expired and they can be safely purged.

2. Gradually extend retention-disposition schedules to all records not covered by general schedules—those that are unique to each office.

3. Make annual visits to each university office to ensure the flow of records from offices to inactive holding areas, to the archives, or to the incinerator as scheduled. It is important to note that we do not have an official records center for inactive records as a part of our system; the expense of erecting and staffing such a facility was prohibitive. Rather than give up the idea of records management, we decided to use part of the archival stack area for the records of key administrative offices that did not have any storage areas. We also encouraged the improvement of the many small storerooms in basements and attics already used by offices. This has been more a compromise than a solution, but it does work and is certainly better than nothing.

4. Establish a series of personnel training sessions involving workshops for clerical staff on basic information retrieval and storage techniques and prepare handbooks for dissemination to clerical staff. The goal of the training is to enable staff to class files in ways that will facilitate appraisal and weeding and to clarify for staff transmittal procedures and the preparation of finding aids for records transferred to the archives.

5. Make regular, periodic visits to university offices, aiding and advising clerical and administrative staff in the implementation of efficient record-retrieval systems and records-storage techniques. Be on call to work with individual offices on record-keeping problems, including reorganization of filing systems and use of filing equipment.

6. In coordination with office staffs, the facilities planning office, and university maintenance, encourage the safe, efficient development and use of office storage areas.

7. Coordinate the development of a university vital-records policy and program. Assign priority in the program to security microfilming of student records maintained by registrars.

8. Encourage the adoption of uniform record-keeping systems in university units with similar functions, such as academic departments, personnel offices, deans' and masters' offices in the residential colleges, and the registrar's offices. Compliance in implementing model filing schemes would be voluntary, leaving staffs free to adjust model systems to the particular conditions of their offices.

9. Coordinate the planning of microfilm conversion projects in those offices of the university that currently maintain records of permanent administrative and research value. Advise university offices that are dealing with

commercial filming and records-storage firms. Develop a university micro-forms application handbooks and workshops for administrative and clerical staff to enable them to make an informed judgment when choosing records to be microfilmed, identifying format, considering costs, drawing up a work plan for the conversion operation, and so forth.

Conclusion

The completion of the records survey marked a major turning point for the Department of Manuscripts and Archives. The data gathered during the survey have enabled us to assess our problems and to plan effective solu-tions. The university's decision to fund the archives/records-management program represents a strong commitment to carrying out these solutions. It is our hope that our experience with the use of records-management tech-niques to reorganize a university archives program will be of value to other institutions in similar circumstances.

Notes

1. Society of American Archivists, College and University Archives Committee, Subcommittee on Standards, *Guidelines for College and Uni-versity Archives* (Chicago: Society of American Archivists, 1982).

2. H.G. Jones, *The Records of a Nation* (New York: Athenaeum, 1969), pp. 189–207.

Appendix 2A:
Increase in Paperwork
Production in Three
University Offices

41

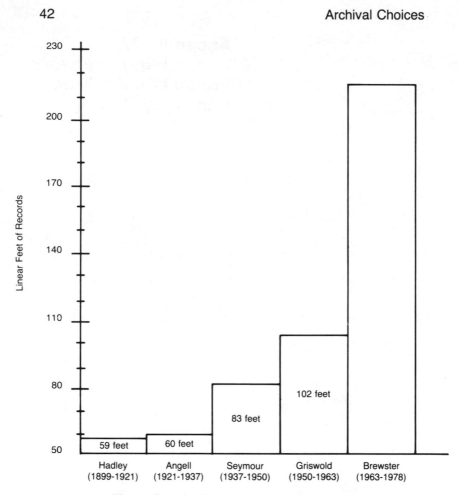

Figure 2A–1. Yale University Presidents

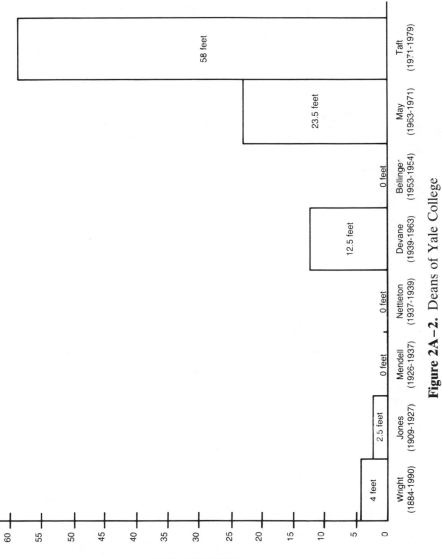

Figure 2A–2. Deans of Yale College

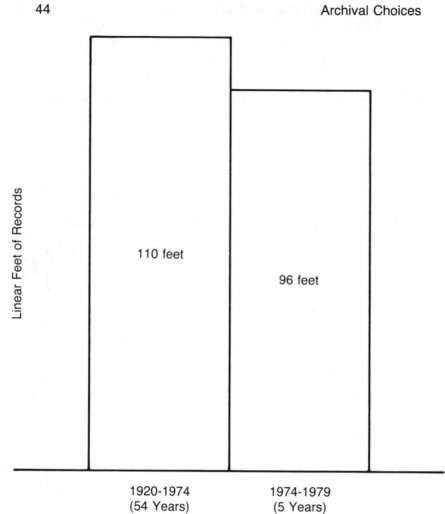

Figure 2A–3. Provost

Appendix 2B: Campus-Wide Survey Forms

Record Series Inventory Report

1. Date: 2. Prepared by:

3. College or Other Primary Units: 4. Division:

5. Office Title: 6. Office Address:

7. Department Head: 8. Liaison: 9. Phone:

10. Name of Record Series: 11. Inclusive Dates:

12. Primary Use of Series:

13. Content of Series:

14. Linear Feet: 15.   Number of File Drawers:

16. Present   Location   of   Series: [] office   [] archives
        [] other storage area:

17. Form of Records: [] paper [] card   [] bound volume   [] microform
        [] machine readable   [] other:

18. Size of Records: [] letter   [] legal   [] other:

19. Type of Storage Equipment: [] file cabinet   [] transfer file   [] lateral file
        [] card file   [] box   [] other:

20. Status of Records: [] original   [] copy
    [] if copy, office of origin:

21. Arrangement of Series:
    Alphabetical by: _____
    Chronological by: _____
    Numerical by: _____
    Organizational by: _____
    Other: _____

22. Access Guide to Series: [] no [] yes
    If so, what type:

23. Annual Accumulation of Records:

24. Delineation of File Breaks (if any):

25. Frequency of Referral to Series:
[] daily [] 1-4x/week [] 1-4x/month
[] 1-10x/year [] less than 1x/year
[] occasionally

26. Percent of Series One Year Old or Less:

Frequency of referral: [] daily
[] 1-4x/week []1-4x/month
[] 1-10x/year []less than 1x/year
[] occasionally

27. Percent of Series More than One Year Old:

Frequency of referral: [] daily
[] 1-4x/week []1-4x/month
[] 1-10x/year [] less than 1x/year
[] occasionally

28. Time Period Series Is Retained in Office:

29. Present Office Procedure for Disposal of Series: [] destroyed   [] archives
    [] other storage:

30. Difficulties Retrieving Records?

31. Is This Series Duplicated? [] never [] sometimes [] often

32. Number of Xerox Machines in Office:

33. In-House Publications and Reports?   [] do not exist   [] report   [] publication
    Frequency of issue:
    Circulation:

34. Number of Cabinets in Office:

35. Additional Comments (use reverse side if necessary):

36. Mss. & A Retention Recommendation:

37. Inventory Reviewed By:

Directions for Completing Survey Form

1. Date the inventory is taken: year, month, day.
2. Name (or initials) of person preparing the form.
3. Name of major academic or major administrative office: for example, Yale college, vice-president of finance.
4. Department or secondary groups: for example, history; bursar. *This may be blank.*
5. Name of place being surveyed.
6. Campus address; include name of building, street address, and zip code.
7. Administrator/chairman/supervisor.
8. Name and title of person in charge of the files: for example, administrative assistant, secretary.
9. Liaison's phone number.
10. This is an important item. If the office staff has a title for the series already, use that. If there is no established title, cooperate with the staff and create one which clearly describes the series. For example: Personnel Files (classified employees) or Student Evaluations of Courses and Instructors.
11. Date of earliest record in the series—date of latest record in the series, if complete. Leave it open if the series is ongoing: for example, 1968- .
12. What is the most important reason for utilizing and maintaining this series? An open question. Add any information that will help explain the existence of the series. *Do not* describe content in this question.
13. Precisely as possible state what is in each series. For example: a series entitled Scheduling and Enrollment Records was described as containing class schedules, records of faculty load and assignment, faculty course and time procedures, final class lists, and enrollment statistics. Also include information explaining why the record is found at its present location, "submitted by" or "sent to" another office, that is, its procedural significance. List of possible terms:

Address Files	Notes (specify)
Applications	Payroll
Bills	Personnel (specify)
Books	Plans
Cases or Case Files	Programs, Special
Correspondence (specify)	Projects
Contracts	Receipts
Convenience Files (specify of what)	Releases
Course Records	Reports (specify)
Curriculum	Requests
Decisions	Research Files

Faculty (specify)	Statements
Grants	Student Records
Inventories and Control	Subject Correspondence
Ledgers	Technical Reference File
Lists	Telephone Numbers
Minutes	Vouchers

14. Total number of feet of records in the series. 1 drawer=2 ft. Use tape measure if necessary.
15. Total number of file drawers for the series.
16. Where are the records? Are they all in the office? Check the appropriate box. Be sure to specify the locations. It is possible for all three boxes to be checked. *Note*: if some of series is located in other storage area, note the inclusive dates of those records in this space.
17. Check the appropriate box. If card, specify type and size: for example, 5×7 index card. If machine readable, specify type: for example, computer tape, punch card.
18. Check appropriate box. If "other," measure and note.
19. Check appropriate box. Indicate size: for example, file cabinet, letter; file cabinet, legal.
20. Check appropriate box. Noting the office of origin is very important.
21. Specify. Note the subarrangements within each type of arrangement.
22. Check the appropriate box. If yes, specify type. Types include: indexes, file guides, registers, explanations of the numerical system.
23. How much is added to the series each year? Include liaison's estimation of volume increase (if possible).
24. Is there a time (for example, the end of calendar or fiscal year) when the office stops filing material in an old file and begins new files?
25. How often are these records referred to overall? (Liaison's approximation.)
26. Obtain from the staff an approximate percentage of the record series which is one year old or less. In addition get a staff approximation of the frequency of use of these records.
27. Obtain from the staff an approximate percentage of the records series which is more than one year old. In addition, get a staff approximation of the frequency of use of these records.
NOTE: questions 26 and 27 are concerned with the currency of the records most often referred to by the staff. Survey form may be altered to indicate this.
28. What is the current policy for preserving the records? How long are they physically present in the office before they are moved to another location? Any information about the disposal should be included in question 29.

29. What is the current policy on disposing of the record series? Specify other storage area.
30. Does the staff have any trouble obtaining information under its current filing and/or disposal system? Can information be located quickly and easily?
31. Indicate which series are duplicated (for dispersal, reference, and so forth). How often and approximately how much material does this entail?
32. Indicate number of Xerox (or other type of photocopy) machines in office.
33. Does the office issue and circulate any reports or publications (such as newsletters, annual reports, and so forth)? If so, how often are they issued? To whom are they issued, for example, department members, administration, separate mailing list?
34. Indicate number of cabinets in office. (This can be a rough estimate.)
35. Use this space for any additional information which will provide a better understanding of the material.
36. To be completed by manuscripts and archives staff.
37. Initials of the reviewer.

Appendix 2C:
Internal Survey Form

University Archives Survey (Record Group:_____)

Collection Title   Dates:

Location: room:_____   range:_____   section:_____   shelf:_____
Folios: room:_____   range:_____   section:_____   shelf:_____

Quantity:
archive boxes: _____	card boxes: _____
1/2 archive boxes: ___	folios: _____
Paige boxes: _____	volumes: _____
black boxes: _____	other: _____

Total linear feet: _____

Record Description:
corres: _____	memorabilia: ___
financial: _____	printed: _____
mss: _____	reports: _____
	other: _____

Status:
- accessioned: _____
- unprocessed: _____
- prelim. inventory: _____
- processed: _____
- finding aid: _____

Condition:

Problems/Recommendations:

                            Initials: Date:

_____

Appendix 2D: Archives Program Statements

Yale University Archives
Statement of Core Mission

1. To appraise, collect, organize, describe, preserve, and make available university records of permanent administrative, legal, fiscal, and historical value.
2. To provide adequate facilities for the retention, preservation, servicing, and research use of such records.
3. To serve as a research center for the study of the university's history by members of the university and the scholarly community at large.
4. To provide information services to assist in the university's administration and operations.
5. To serve in a public-relations capacity by promoting knowledge and understanding of the origins, programs, and goals of the university and their development.
6. To facilitate the efficient management of the recorded information produced by the university's units and offices.

Yale University Archives
Collection Policy Statement

As part of its core mission, the university archives is charged with the collection and maintenance of those university records possessing permanent administrative, legal, fiscal, and historical value. Determination of the status of a university record is based upon an informed appraisal of the record's value by the appropriate university officers and administrators.

The decision to preserve records for administrative, legal, and fiscal purposes is the responsibility of the university's permanent officers and administrators and should be made in consultation with the university archivist. In general, these decisions are embodied in the university's governing and by-laws and in its records-retention and disposition schedules.

The decision to select and preserve records of historical value is the responsibility of the university archivist. The purpose of collecting such

Department of Manuscripts and Archives, Yale University Library, May 1980. Printed with permission.

53

records is to provide documentation of the development and growth of the university, particularly of its primary functions of teaching and research, its role in the community at large, the activities of its student body, and the development of its physical plant and grounds. Priority is given to those records that reflect the activities of university officers who and committees that formulate or approve university or divisionwide policy as well as faculty and administrative involvement in these activities.

Yale University Archives
Record-Appraisal Guidelines

1. Are the records official university records or records produced by a university-related organization, group, or individual?
2. Are the records covered by retention-disposition schedules?
3. Do the records have permanent legal, administrative, fiscal, historical, or public-relations value?
4. If the significance of the records is solely historical, does it fall within the archives' collecting policy? For example, do the records document an aspect of the university's growth and development, particularly its primary functions of teaching and research, its role in the community at large, the activities of its student body, or the development of its physical plant and grounds?
5. Do similar records exist elsewhere? That is, is the document an official copy of a record from the office of origin or is it a duplication of the copy of record?
6. If similar records exist, are they:
   a. Available?
   b. More authoritative, more nearly complete, or a summarization of the essential information?
   c. In a more desirable arrangement?
   d. More desirable in terms of preservation?
7. What are the restrictions on the records?
8. Does the historical value of the records warrant the level of processing procedures necessary to preserve the records and make them available for research?

Yale Minimum-Level Processing
Standards for University Archives

The goal of processing records in the university archives is to facilitate the records' use by a broad range of researchers—university administrators, historians and social scientists, students, alumni, and others—approaching the records with different interests and from varying points of view. The primary use of the records will no doubt continue to be by researchers studying the development and growth of the university, particularly its primary functions of teaching and research, its role in the community at large, the activities of its student body, and the development of its physical plant. But, in addition, the records are of value to researchers investigating the whole spectrum of social, cultural, intellectual, and political history, including the history of higher education in the United States, fine arts, science, minorities, and women. Finding aids must be prepared with these needs in mind.

We are making an effort to establish a basic, minimum level of control and description for all records now in the archives as well as for all future accessions. Certain records will warrant more elaborate subject descriptions but *all* will *at least* meet the following standards.

I. Description
    A. A register format-finding aid will be prepared for each accession of records and will include the following information:
        1. Name of office of origin.
        2. Date accession was received by the archives.
        3. Broad summary description of type of records, for example, "student files, arranged alphabetically by class year," "alphabetically arranged subject-correspondence file," and so forth.
        4. Broad subject areas of potential research value; purpose of records and function they document, if not apparent.
        5. Inclusive dates of records.
        6. Number and type of boxes.
        7. A file-folder listing of the records.
        8. Name of person preparing the finding aid.

II. Physical Control
    A. All records will be stored in appropriate type of archival-quality container, for instance, Paige boxes or manuscript boxes.
    B. All containers will be labeled with archives self-adhering labels containing the following information (and all information on labels should be typewritten):
        1. Name of office of origin.
        2. Date of accession.
        3. Archives record-group number.
        4. Sequential number of boxes, for example, 1, 2, 3, 4, and so on.
    C. All folders will be numbered with box and folder number, full record-group number, and accession date. For example:

	YRG 21	A	10	3/80	Accession Date
	Divinity School	Dean's Office		Dean Leander Keck	

III. Arrangement of Records
   A. Accessions of archival records will normally be described and pre-
      served in the order in which they were created and maintained in
      the office of origin.

   B. In cases where no order exists or none is readily apparent, the
      records should be arranged in an order that will facilitate the expedi-
      tious retrieval of information by the archives' staff and researchers.
      1. Generally, establishing this order will involve putting folders
         into chronological or alphabetical order and grouping records by
         subject (and chronologically or alphabetically within subject
         area) or into units by record form or type, for example, financial
         and accounting records, correspondence, subject files, commit-
         tee files, reports.
IV. Conservation Procedures
   A. Remove all rubber bands.
   B. Remove staples, paper clips, and other hardware *only* when they
      are rusty, extremely numerous, or large.
   C. Flag low-quality paper for preservation photocopying.
D. Refolder material only when folders are in poor condition, for
   example, with tabs breaking off.

Appendix 2E: Sources of Further Information on Records Management

Benedon, William. *Records Management*. Englewood Cliffs, NJ: Prentice-Hall, 1969.

Blegen, August H. *Records Management Step-by-Step*. Stamford, CT: Office Publications Inc., 1965.

Griffin, Mary Claire. *Records Management: A Modern Tool for Business*. Boston: Allyn and Bacon, 1964.

Kahn, Gilbert, et al. *Progressive Filing and Records Management*. New York: McGraw-Hill, 1962.

Leahy, Emmett J. and Cameron, Christopher A. *Modern Records Management*. New York: McGraw-Hill, 1965.

Maedke, Wilmer O., Robek, Mary F., and Brown, Gerald F. *Information and Records Management*. Beverly Hills, CA: Glencoe Press, 1974.

Periodicals

Administrative Management, 212 Fifth Avenue, New York, NY 10010

American Archivist, 330 S. Wells Street, Suite 810, Chicago, IL 60606

Business Automation, 288 Park Avenue West, Elmhurst, IL 60126

Information and Records Management, 101 Crossways Park West, Woodbury, NY 11797

Journal of Data Management, 505 Busse Highway, Park Ridge, IL 60068

Microfilm Techniques, 101 Crossways Park West, Woodbury, NY 11797

Records Management Quarterly, 4200 Somerset, Suite 215, Prairie Village, KS 66208

The Secretary, National Secretaries Assoc., 616 East 63rd Street, Kansas City, MO 64110

Government Documents: NARS-GSA Records-Management Handbooks

Managing Current Files

Files Operation, 1964, 022-002-00013-9

Department of Manuscripts and Archives, Yale University Library. Printed with permission.

Files Stations, 1967, 022-002-00012-1
Subject Filing, 1966

Managing Information Retrieval

Computer Output Microfilm, 1975, 022-001-00069-8
Information Retrieval, 1972, 022-002-00036-8
Information Retrieval Systems, 1970, 022-002-00030-9
Microfilming Records, 1974, 022-001-00033-3

Managing the Mail

Managing the Mail, 1971, 022-002-00033-3

Managing Noncurrent Files

Applying Records Schedules, 1961
Federal Records Centers, 1967
General Records Schedules, 1976

Managing Forms

Forms Analysis, 1960, 022-002-00015-5
Forms Design, 1960, 022-002-00028-7
Forms Management, 1969, 022-002-00014-7

Managing Correspondence

Correspondence Management, 1973, 022-003-00899-3
Form and Guide Letters, 1973, 022-003-00903-5

Professional Associations

Association of Records Managers and Administrators, 4200 Somerset, Suite
    215, Prairie Village, KS 66208
Business Equipment Manufacturer's Association, 235 East 42nd Street,
    New York, NY 10037

Data Processing Management Association, 505 Busse Highway, Park Ridge, IL 60068

National Microfilm Association, Suite 1101, 8728 Colesville Road, Silver Springs, MD 20910

National Office Product Association, 1500 Wilson Boulevard, Arlington, VA 22209

National Secretaries Association, 616 East 63rd Street, Kansas City, MO 64110

Society of American Archivists, 330-South Wells Street, Suite 810, Chicago, IL 60606

3

An Agenda for
the Appraisal of
Business Records

Francis X. Blouin, Jr.

To tackle the entire range of problems associated with the appraisal of business records in one chapter is no small task. A century ago, it might have been possible to give brief guidelines, but, with the explosive growth of the number of companies and the emergence of a small fraction of those companies as large, multinational enterprises, it is quickly apparent that the phrase "appraisal of business records" understates the complexity of the appraisal problem. Firms faced with warehouses full of records long for guidelines and formulas that would provide easily administered solutions to sifting, weeding, and choosing the permanent record. The unaware or uninformed still cry for the retention of all records. The narrow-minded, on the other hand, are inclined to destroy all records and tracks to the past. Simple, or even complex, guidelines have yet to appear.

One chapter cannot deliver any specific formula or solution, but it can elaborate on the parameters of the appraisal problem as it relates to business records. In so doing, this chapter will review the environment from which the current concern for the research use of business records has arisen and then focus briefly on the current climate. In conclusion, an agenda for considering the problems of the appraisal of business records will be offered. Some general points about the problem of appraisal and how to best address it in the years ahead will also be discussed.

Awareness of the historical importance of business records came rather late in the course of the development of archival sources in the United States. When archivists and historians did begin to define business history as a discipline, interest in business records became particularly intense. Early historical societies concentrated largely on material deemed historical. Collections assembled during the nineteenth century at the Massachusetts, New York, and other early historical societies included material relating to business enterprise and entrepreneurs but did not reflect any systematic awareness of the role of business, institutions, finance, and capitalism in the growth of the early republic.[1] In the late nineteenth century, after the founding of the American Historical Association (AHA), historians became professionally concerned about the condition of historical records in the United States. This led to the now-famous AHA surveys of state records and the international surveys of historical documentation funded by the Car-

61

negie Endowment for International Peace.[2] These important reports focused on public records, underscoring the researcher's preoccupation with the political and diplomatic aspects of the national history. Little attention was given to business records until the Business Historical Society in Cambridge, Massachusetts, was founded in 1925 for the purpose of encouraging and aiding the "study of the evolution of business in all periods and in all countries."[3] Early records of the society describe the members' intense efforts to locate a variety of business records with an eye to document the U.S. business experience. These efforts coincided with the first formal attempts to establish business history as a specialized field of historical research, as well as with early attempts to define business administration as an academic and professional field of inquiry. From the perspective of appraisal, the most interesting facet of the work of the Business Historical Society is its indication of the society's confidence that comprehensive documentation of the U.S. business experience could be located, preserved, and made available.[4]

Though enthusiasm remained high, this confidence could not be maintained. Very quickly, historians and archivists of the time came to realize that special problems were associated with the collection of historical business records. In 1929, the American Council of Learned Societies set up, in cooperation with the Social Science Research Council, a Joint Committee on Materials for Research. Some years later, in the middle 1930s, the American Library Association began to include the problem of gathering business records on the agenda of its Committee on Archives and Libraries. Little of a concrete nature came from these meetings.[5] The mere existence of these forums, however, suggests the early awareness of obstacles to adequate documentation of U.S. business. The only work to specifically address the problem of appraisal was that of Ralph M. Hower, who prepared a pamphlet, *The Preservation of Business Records*, for the Business Historical Society in 1937. This pamphlet was the first formal and systematic attempt to assist archivists in determining what should be saved from the bulk of business records generated by the modern company.[6]

Hower's "governing principle in selecting business records for historical purposes" was to "choose material which will yield accurate and reasonably complete information about every phase of the business—production, distribution, management, finances, personnel, accounting, and plant."[7] His categories would be familiar to today's archivist: summary data were preferred to daily vouchers and logs; formal ledgers and daybooks were preferred to wastebooks and cancelled checks. There were two problems with Hower's analysis. First, its scope was so broad that, ultimately, it argued that nearly everything should be saved. His concerns were all-inclusive: summary accounting data, including samples of all forms used; purchasing information, including papers relating to methods and policies, items and quantities, and sources of supply and prices paid; production information, including all data relating to plant operation and design, and all material that indicates what a firm makes and how it is made; records relating to personnel and labor relations, including material that describes the character of the work force and includes supervisory information on hiring, accident reports, and other aspects of policy; sales information in summary form that not only gives aggregate figures but also illustrates shipping demand, sales promotion, selling expenses, and so forth. He was particularly concerned that the records of the statistics department be retained to explain why certain figures were generated. Of course, minutes and official records as well as all correspondence of high-level executives were to be retained.[8] He supplemented his recommendations with a series of interesting case studies. In his analysis, he recognized the problem of bulk in the preservation of business records. In his concern for the documentation of all aspects of a business operation, however, he ended up recommending the retention of a considerable portion of the records, far more than archivists can realistically hope to retain today.

The second problem with Hower's analysis was that it focused exclusively on the individual firm. Thus, for Hower, operational records were particularly important because how a firm functioned became the critical question. Later literature in the field would suggest broader historical concerns regarding business climate, business culture, and other more sweeping questions. These particular themes were not widely recognized as central to the concerns of business history in the 1920s and 1930s and thus were not considered in this formal analysis of business records.

Though the Hower pamphlet did not provide a long-term solution to the problem of appraising business records, much of the early work sponsored by the Business Historical Society indicated that the society was, in many ways, a model archival enterprise. Scholars in the field met regularly with business executives, librarians, and curators, and together they worked to both define business history as a specific field of historical inquiry and collect historical records to ensure that research resources to sustain that field would be permanently available. From these early efforts, the Business Manuscripts Collection at the Baker Library, Harvard University, was established.

By the 1940s, the archival interests of the society had given way to a more focused interest on specific questions relating to business history. The thrill of discovering eighteenth- and nineteenth-century banking, textile, and other business records quickly gave way to concern regarding the problem of dealing with bulky late-nineteenth-century and early-twentieth-century records. The Hower piece was designed to help archivists come to grips with the problem, but businesses were growing in size and complexity even as he wrote.

    Sensing the difficulties involved in the preservation and care of business records, in the early 1940s, the editor of the *Journal of Economic History* asked Arthur Cole, librarian of the Harvard Business School, to reflect on developments in the handling of business manuscripts.[9] His article, "The Accumulated Development of Unsolved Problems," presented an analysis of the problems of collecting and preserving the records of business firms that still rings true today.[10] Cole had been instrumental in developing the archival interests of the Business Historical Society and had worked with Dean Edwin Gay of the Harvard Business School in establishing the Baker Library Business Manuscripts Collection.

    In his analysis of the problem of business records, Cole saw two distinct problems: "the bulk of physical quantity of recent business records, and the lack of mechanism for equating scholar's demands with librarians' supplies."[11] In recent years, the problem of bulk has been discussed primarily in terms of the records of the public sector. Yet, decades ago, the Business Historical Society recognized and wrestled with the bulk problem in terms of business records. In the late 1940s, Cole countered his own concerns about the bulk of historical business records with the thought that "somehow libraries and historical societies will be able to give sanctuary to the manuscript survivals of interest to the economic historian *other* than business records."[12] Similarly, he argued that it would not be unrealistic to "assume that the business records relating to the period roughly antedating 1890 will find a resting place in university libraries or other archival repositories."[13] The problem, then, was the flood of paper generated by modern business. Cole despaired that such records could be preserved in any systematic way within the confines of traditional archival repositories. His reasons will sound familiar. He was concerned with: (1) bulk; (2) possibility that the codes and symbols of modern accounting methods would render much financial data wholly unintelligible to all but those most intimately aware of the inner workings of a company; and (3) the general lack of use the materials would receive in relation to the cost of their storage. He also doubted the accepted view of the time that summary information would essentially be a capsule of the information contained in the bulk of the records. Although he noted the efforts over 140 repositories in the United States were making to acquire large collections, it was clear to him that even the boldest acquisition attempts would only provide documentation for a small, almost miniscule, proportion of the total U.S. business experience. He further noted that even those materials that were accessioned often were not processed properly for scholarly research.[14]

    Cole's recognition of these problems led him to another concern: that the research done by scholars interested in business history would be imbalanced, largely because the parameters of their inquiries were often limited by whatever information repositories were able to acquire. While Cole could then have gone on to speculate about the kinds of material libraries should seek to acquire, his awareness of the bulk problem led him to the conclusion that, if the records of business enterprises were to be preserved, the business community itself would have to take the lead. The early experience of the Business History Society probably fueled Cole's optimism for this approach. Many executives shared the aims of the society and were working to establish corporate archives. The so-called Clough-Cochran method, developed by Shepard B. Clough, then of Columbia University, and Thomas C. Cochran, then of New York University, further increased Cole's optimism. Clough and Cochran developed a well-conceived argument to make businesses aware of the cost advantages of organized archives. They appealed to the business instinct for balanced histories, restricted access, and bottom-line cost analysis. Cochran and Clough envisioned their method's offering a solution that would satisfy the interests of both scholars and businessmen. While the method did not, in fact, offer a solution, it did offer hope, and it was the only realistic way Cole could find to respond to the seemingly unsolvable problem raised by his own analysis. He hoped for continued concern on the part of historians, archivists, and librarians, but he saw their roles as ones concentrated on guiding the efforts of private enterprise to solve its own problems.[15] Thus, with regard to the appraisal problem, Cole could respond only with a vision, not a solution:

> But if we must select, and if in the face of the present-day mountains of business records we can hope to preserve only a small percentage, even with the aid of beneficiently co-operative companies, we may properly ask certain questions. On what basis shall the collectors of documents proceed and with what objectives in their several regions shall future apostles of activity by companies lay their campaigns? Is there no way by which the guild of economic and business historians can block out a minimum scheme and set up some central body with the several objectives: first, to ascertain what portion of this scheme is already accomplished or in the way of fulfillment; thereafter to act as a clearinghouse of information upon current activities; and perhaps to give advice—if and when asked—upon the problems that now confront libraries and historical societies and that may well perplex local missionary groups in subsequent years?[16]

The Cole article represented a bench mark of sorts in the evolution of thought about business records. Cole was likely aware of two facets of this bench mark; the third was probably less obvious to him. First, the article provided a summary statement of the role of the Business Historical Society in the preservation of business records. Nearly twenty years prior to the publication of his article, Cole and others had launched an intensive and broad-based effort to document a particular aspect of U.S. history. From its first grand vision through nearly twenty years of collecting, the society immersed itself in archival concerns. By 1945, all that work had come to a virtual halt, mired in the recognition that no practical solution to the appraisal problem could be found and that truly adequate documentation could never be housed within the confines of academically oriented repositories.

The second facet of the bench mark related to the appearance of the article in the *Journal of Economic History*. In fact, the article was requested by the *Journal* in the belief that business records were an important source, not only for the business historian, but for economic historians as well. This fusion of interests led to a broad-based scholarly constituency supporting efforts to preserve business records. In an era when historians focused on institutions, the business firm was recognized as a critically important power. Thus, in writing the history of the economy from the institutional perspective, leading scholars could not help but be concerned about the condition of business records.

The third facet of the bench mark Cole's article represented was, in fact, the other side of the second. During the postwar era, the growth of government became an accepted fact. The ever-increasing presence of government in all aspects of U.S. life led, among other things, to a preoccupation with statistics. This trend, coupled with the rise of social science, meant that many aspects of U.S. history formerly studied individually on the basis of specific institutional histories now could be approached in an aggregate way through the use of statistics based on theoretical models. This created, on the one hand, a gradual separation of the interests of economic historians and those of traditional business historians and, on the other, an expansion of both groups' concerns beyond the history of specific institutions to broader questions of policy and political philosophy. Thus, the strong coalition of interests that argued for resources (both financial and intellectual) to collect and preserve the records of U.S. business history began to break apart along disciplinary and methodological lines. Concurrently, the postwar economic boom, much of which benefited U.S. corporations, led to an expansion the like of which no economy had ever seen. For the United States, this resulted in, among other things, megacorporations generating records of such bulk that, even if saved, no scholar could grasp in the course of a lifetime.

Throughout the 1950s and the 1960s, interest in business records continued to ebb and flow with one of a number of high points being the establishment of the Henry Ford Archives in Dearborn, Michigan.[17] The Business Archives Committee of the Society of American Archivists continued to work to coordinate and publicize efforts to collect and preserve business records, both by businesses and by research-oriented repositories. The question of appraisal was raised, but little of this dialogue ever reached print.

One exception was an article by Robert Lovett, curator of the Baker Library collection, on "The Appraisal of Older Business Records." In the article, Lovett discussed the procedures he had used to appraise specific collections of New England textile firms. These were, for the most part, very large collections that had been stored unprocessed at Baker for some years.[18] In preparing the collection for research, he generally followed the Hower guidelines, careful to retain segments of the records that would cover as many aspects of the firm's activities as possible. Only miscellaneous receipts, checks, and other ephemeral materials were discarded. In his 1952 article, Lovett introduced the concept of retaining a reasonable sample of records as another solution to the business-records bulk problem. In his work at Baker, he had, in some cases, retained select types of documents at ten-year intervals, resulting in considerable space savings. In the 1970s, archivists at the University of Michigan adapted Lovett's sampling techniques when processing collections of nineteenth- and early-twentieth-century lumber records, eliminating a considerable percentage of total holdings.[19] Neither of these projects involved scientific sampling; in fact, scientific sampling was rejected as inappropriate to the nature of the material. Rather, in each case, the samples retained were a judicious selection of material that would give a profile or overview of the company at specific points in time—both preserving a horizontal perspective over time and providing a periodic vertical perspective into all aspects of corporate operations as reflected in the records from which the samples were taken.

In the 1980s, archivists responsible for business records have Hower and the sampling literature to provide guidelines on how large business collections might be handled. In addition, of course, there is the theoretical literature referred to by Professor Peace at the beginning of this book. Yet the appraisal problem remains. Now, nearly forty years after the publication of the Cole and Cochran articles, might we still conclude that business manuscripts continue to be a pressing problem? The response must be yes, though there are encouraging signs.

For an encouraging sign that large corporate collections are being preserved, one need only look at those companies that have taken on the responsibility of providing staff and facilities for an open corporate archives. Robert Levey, writing in *Dun's Review*, noted that 201 U.S. business firms have archival programs, and he proclaimed, the "history of American business is alive and well."[20] A number of those companies developed their programs some years ago, indicating a genuine commitment to research-oriented archives.[21]

However, if one uses the purely theoretical definition of archives, which includes any systematic attempt on the part of an institution to preserve its own records for whatever reason, the number of existing archives rises considerably, to the point where a precise count is impossible to determine.

Consider, for example, that the membership of the Association of Records Managers and Administrators is now approaching 7,500 people, with a considerable percentage of that membership in the private sector. Those records managers are maintaining archives, perhaps not open for public use or for research, but archives nonetheless. These are systematic programs designed to both preserve the vital historical corporate record and maintain those records in immediate administrative use. Great care and attention has been given to many of the record groups considered particularly vital to particular institutions. The trend toward using underground salt mines for storage and making a considerable investment in micrographics speaks to the clear commitment on the part of corporations to maintain their archives.

Two forces, corporation size and federal regulations, have worked to encourage corporations to maintain documentation of one sort or another. If the booth of a corner fruit-stand operator was burned to the ground, it is likely that the operator would have most of his vital corporate information in his head and could easily open another stand the next day. On the other hand, if a similar fate struck the headquarters of the United Fruit Company and if that facility housed the only archives of the company, the reconstitution of that corporate record would be a much more difficult task. Size, then, can encourage rather than discourage record keeping. In an earlier article, the author has explored this idea, essentially concluding that, as institutions become more complex, the requirements for record keeping change. In general increased complexity results in an increase rather than a decrease in the amount of documentation generated.[22] Thus, greater size leads to the use of both systems for corporate communication and systematic programs for the management of the records that result.

A second, more recent motivation for records retention on the part of private industry has been the various regulatory programs of the federal government. The *Federal Register* now lists thousands of regulations for the preparation of various kinds of records, varying from well-known environmental-impact studies to specific, lesser-known records requirements for ginners of cotton, crushers of castor beans, importers of non-human primates, contractors for the construction of public airports, and others. These regulations have served to induce corporations to create records that they might otherwise neglect to produce. The convergence of size and government regulation, then, have served to encourage, rather than discourage, the creation of records. Thus, one aspect of the Clough-Cochran vision for corporate archives has been confirmed—that corporations would find it in their best interest to retain records and, in effect, establish their own archives.[23]

What does this encouragement suggest with regard to the question of appraisal? Clearly, records are being retained, but which records? The necessity to retain records, coupled with the propensity of large corporations to generate considerable paper, has raised the question of appraisal in many corporate offices and boardrooms. One need only look at the records-management literature to see that corporate appraisal decisions are reflected in the retention and disposition schedules being prepared daily. The appraisal guidelines popular in corporate circles are determined largely by two factors: (1) the climate of litigation in modern U.S. society; and (2) federal and state government regulations. Fear of litigation is, to some extent, an inducement to save, but, to a greater extent, it is an incentive to destroy records. Apart from contracts that most attorneys suggest be kept in perpetuity, and with the exception of data vital to the continued basic functioning of a corporation—however that may be defined—there is little inducement for corporate staff to save. For now, the only external inducement, other than the corporation's desire to be of public service, are the myriad of state and federal regulations that require not only the creation of a record but also its retention. These regulations pertain for the most part to regularly kept records, such as employee, product, and financial data.

From a positive perspective, the amount of activity in the area of records management and records monitoring, coupled with enormous growth in the size of corporations and increased interest by government in the creation and retention of records, has served to encourage the development of systematically managed corporate archives.

Also from the positive perspective, one must cite the enormous efforts of many research repositories to preserve the early records of U.S. business enterprises. Notable among these is, in addition to the Baker Library at Harvard, the Eleutherian Mills Historical Library in Greenville, Delaware. Both collections specialize in the business history of their respective regions. Other large repositories have also worked to assemble business records to the extent that they fit the collecting themes of the respective institutions. The State Historical Society of Wisconsin, the California Historical Society, the Bentley Historical Library, among many other institutions, have, over the years, worked to acquire early business records. The efforts of these institutions have made available considerable documentation relating to business before 1890. Again, Cole's prediction that academic repositories could conceivably house extant business records prior to that date has proved correct. It is in the more recent periods that collecting has become more difficult. Due partly to the unavailability of modern business records and partly to the bulk of those record groups that are available, research-oriented repositories find that they have neither the budget nor the space to continue to document the workings of U.S. business enterprises in the twentieth century in the way they documented enterprises in the nineteenth and earlier centuries.

One could be encouraged by the fact that an enormous amount of material is being saved. A record of U.S. business exists in some form for nearly all sectors of the economy. There is, however, a negative aspect to the current state of business records.

From the perspective of research-oriented archives, corporate records, though extant, remain closed, and the records-management methods by which they are assembled is questionable. The result of the problems with the records, and other problems within the academic fields of business and economic history, is that the appraisal question has been set in parameters too narrow to ensure adequate documentation for the future. The sum of these problems underscore the pressing nature of the business-manuscripts problem.

The closed nature of corporate archives represents a clear problem. When Clough and Cochran developed their methodology nearly thirty-five years ago, they envisioned that corporations would welcome serious researchers and make their archival material readily available. That, however, has been the case in only a very few companies. Douglas Bakken, director of the Henry Ford Archives, has rightly pointed out that few corporate archives or records centers meet the guidelines for business archives suggested by the Society of American Archivists.[24] This fact raises questions about the effects of corporate appraisal decisions on the long-term interests of historical research. Few enterprises see the service of scholarship as a part of their general records-management program. In most cases, records management is done simply because it is cost effective, and it is motivated by the legal requirement that a record of corporate activity be preserved.

The state of the disciplines that archives primarily serve poses another problem. Although all persons interested in business archives are not necessarily professional business historians, the disciplines of business and economic history make particularly relevant demands on corporate archives. Collecting policy and appraisal decisions should not be overly influenced by current trends; neither should they ignore the trends. As noted previously, Arthur Cole's article, "Business Manuscripts, A Pressing Problem," represented a convergence of the interests of business historians, economic historians, archivists, and librarians. That convergence has passed. In the years following the publications of Cole's article, economic history has, to a great extent, come to rely on statistical data produced by government sources. The revolutionizing of social-science methodology has encouraged economic historians to move from a primarily institutional focus to one preoccupied with aggregate process. While certain types of business records are still used, scholarship is no longer dominated by those sources that provided the data for the business histories and entrepreneur biographies that were so popular in the past. There is now a methodological cleavage between business and economic history. Even within business history concentration has shifted away from the business firm. Though business historians still retain a more institutional focus, the bulk of research concentrates on aggregate policy, business-government interaction, or the histories of entire industries. There are, of course, many exceptions, the most important being the work of Alfred D. Chandler, Jr. However, from 1977 to 1981 only approximately 7 percent of the authors of articles published in *Business History Review* relied on what might be considered traditional corporate archives. Clearly, there has been a reduced demand for use of corporate records among historians of U.S. business and the economy, and this reduction indicates an erosion of the convergence of academic interest in business archives formed decades ago when business and economic historians shared a common interest and methodology.

Given the problematic status of business records, what should constitute an appropriate agenda for solving the appraisal problem as it relates to business records? The author's view is that archivists should shift their focus from quantity to substance. The universe of available records is currently being defined. Records are being selected in the organization where they are created. The question for archivists is how best to influence the process by which selection decisions are made. Any proposed solution to the appraisal problem for business records must contain five elements: (1) an understanding of the structure of the modern firm; (2) an understanding of the relationship between structure and records generated; (3) an appreciation of the breadth of historical research; (4) a revival of a coalition of interests; and (5) an appreciation of appraisal as an intellectual question.

The key to understanding the records of modern business enterprises rests on an understanding of the structure of the modern company. There is, of course, no one structure that characterizes the myriad of corporate organizations established over the past two centuries. Thus, structural models will have to be developed through a study of extant historical records or from existing studies of each company.[25] The vertical-integration model described by Alfred Chandler is a case in point. What sort of company fits this model? How are the component operations of a vertically integrated company distinctive from separate companies that specialize in a particular single function? Is a vertically integrated company, by definition, a leader in its industry—that is, does vertical integration signify an innovator in a specific industry?[26] Chandler also explored the role of strategy in the structural form of a business enterprise. Is corporate strategy an essential determinant of structural form? If strategy precedes structure, is it necessary to analyze strategy in order to determine structure? Or are the cases Chandler cites atypical of U.S. enterprise?[27] Douglas North and Lance Davis, in exploring the relationship between institutional change and economic growth, have offered a different model for the analysis of institutional structures. North and Davis suggested that structural change in the economy as a whole has important implications for the structures of individual firms. They argued that shifts in the overall structure of the economy affect the innovation, policies, and legal environment of a corporation. How an individual company responds to general shifts in the economy has implications for both its corporate strategies and its structure. To what extent is this theory valid? When critical shifts in the structure of the economy occur, what are the key forms of institutional response? North and Davis suggested that companies might respond to changes in the economy by making specific innovative decisions, voluntarily entering into cooperative decision making with other companies in its industry, or pursuing a specific government action.[28] For the appraisal process, this all suggests a movement away from the consideration of a company's product and location to broader questions of its place in the structural evolution of U.S. business and its centrality to the process of economic growth. If selection must be made, it seems these larger questions will have to be considered. Considerable work must yet be done to further develop our understanding of structural models before they can be used as the basis for evolving an analytical framework for the appraisal problem.

In addition to considering the role of structure in explaining and defining the varieties and types of business firms, archivists interested in the records of business enterprises need to study further the changing functions within specific types. Communication, for example, would be a critical area for analysis. As the form of a business changes, how does its work force communicate within and outside the company? What are the lines of communication? How are the lines of authority drawn? What are the effects of technological change on intracompany communication? All questions related to structural change are of critical consideration in a proper appraisal of corporate records. JoAnne Yates, of the Massachusetts Institute of Technology, is currently studying such critical questions and will offer an important framework for the analysis of internal corporate communication. Michael Lutzker, of New York University, has already offered a sweeping analysis on this subject. Drawing from the work of Max Weber, Lutzker argues that the theory of bureaucratic behavior suggests models of bureaucratic structure. Because all large institutions eventually become bureaucratized to some extent, an understanding of the nature of bureaucracy should lead to a better understanding of the structure of large organizations. Of course, this theme needs to be pursued further. Weberian-based perspectives need more thorough exploration and definition before they can be used to create a framework for formulating appraisal decisions.[29]

The study of structure, then, is critical to understanding the records of business firms. By gaining an understanding of structural types and forms, one can begin to recognize the various organizational forms used to structure human activities, and by analysis of those structures, or the behavior of individuals within the structures, one can begin to ask better questions of the records generated. But the first step is a serious and abstract analysis of structure for its own sake.

A second and separate concern is the relationship of structure to record keeping. Virtually all organized economic activity requires record keeping of some sort or another. When the structure of that activity changes, then the form of record keeping will likely change as well. On one hand, how record keeping affects structure should be considered. To what extent does the form of record keeping and the ability to communicate recorded information limit or define structure? How do evolving systems of record keeping change structure? On the other hand, how does structure affect record keeping? Does growth result in a specialization of the kind of records produced? What function do specific records serve? What is the nature of regularly kept records? And, in keeping with general and traditional concerns, where are decisions made in the "structural" hierarchy and to what extent are those decisions documented?

These are very comprehensive questions, and they require considerable research into the background of modern organizations. Yet, because they are fundamental questions, they must be answered before any material can be selected intelligently. How is an archivist to address this problem? Two approaches seem worth following. The first would be to encourage the undertaking and publication of case studies. When an appraisal of a corporate record group is completed, the findings should be circulated and the nature and result of the study should be described in detail. Such case studies will assist others who are doing selection. The nature of this assistance will improve as a substantive case literature is developed. More important, such analyses would be useful ways to open a dialogue with specific records-management programs that seem particularly ahistorical. This is initially a microapproach, focusing in detail on the relationship of structure to records in one specific company.

A second approach—a macroapproach—would focus on the current environment for record keeping. For this approach, more must be known about statutory requirements for the retention of records. If corporations are saving only what is required, what sort of documentation is being saved? For those companies that follow the letter of the law, what are the appraisal implications of these statutes? This is an area that deserves specific study because it can yield specific conclusions. It is probably futile to think that statutes can be revised so as to require preservation of items of historic value. However, familiarity with the range of statutes will provide a profile of that portion of modern business records mandated by law to survive for a time or in perpetuity.

In addition to an analysis of statutes, a broader study of current retention practices is needed. What sort of material is usually kept? How many
corporations are concerned with keeping records for historical purposes? Is
there an inverse correlation between the size of corporations and their
historical consciousness? To what extent has the current legal environment
served to encourage or discourage record keeping? In addition, it is important to determine when concern about access begins to influence the formulation of records-retention policy. We live in an age that is very records
conscious. Businesses continue to generate enormous amounts of paper, yet
archivists and historians, who have a broad perspective on the function of
historical records, have reason to be suspicious of records-management
procedures and the appraisal decisions made in corporate record centers,
file rooms, and desks. Given the level of records-management activity and
the level of government regulation of business in the United States, the
historical record relating to the structure of U.S. business enterprises is
probably better than one might imagine. Although access to that record
certainly is a problem, the record is there, albeit in bits and pieces. However,
substantive research into the nature of that record is required before we can
authoritatively say the record is thorough and historically useful.

So far, discussion has centered on concerns relating primarily to business as a structural and institutional entity within the context of the U.S.
economy. In the terms of Theodore Schellenberg, these concerns relate to
the evidential side of the appraisal question, and, one might add, they relate
to the functional side as well.[30] Questions have been asked that address the
need to document the role of U.S. business as a system of production and
distribution of goods and services. A third area of concern pertains to the
impact of business on U.S. life and culture. This concern addresses the
informational side of the appraisal question. Thomas C. Cochran summarized the impact of business in a study. From a broadly conceived perspective, he explored the role of business as a social and cultural force: as
educator, as a source of values, as a source of tradition and culture, as an
imperialist, as art, as an instrument of social control, as a force in U.S.
politics, and so forth.[31] These are large issues that cannot be adequately
addressed by research into any individual corporate archives. Yet sources
related to these broad questions must be preserved. Judging from current
historiographical trends, many of these questions can be investigated
through printed material and aggregate data, sources apart from the corporate archival record. The lack of archivally based research is as much a
function of the quantity of corporate records now available in some areas as
of the fact that so much of the corporate record is still restricted. The very
broad and sweeping nature of these larger research questions render them
less useful as a framework of analysis for specific studies of corporate
record keeping. Yet this sort of wide-ranging question increasingly charac-

terizes the work of that segment of the research community interested in business records. Analysis of research trends and historiographical debates, then, remain important to the analysis of records of specific corporate organizations.

If one accepts the idea that most early business records—pre-1900—have found or eventually will find their way into archives of one sort or another, then the researcher's concern focuses on the corporation of this century. Particularly troublesome are the megacorporations whose operations seem so influential in our lives but so incomprehensible. Research into the structures and practices of those companies is very much needed. But, then, of what value is the research if it cannot effect change? Of what value is abstract inquiry if it cannot be applied to specific appraisal problems? These questions suggest yet another area of concern, one regarding whether adequate capacities and strategies exist to ensure the retention of the historical record. Research provides knowledge, awareness, and experience. The case for the preservation and judicious appraisal of business records will be much improved if archivists work to attain a better understanding of the nature and process of record keeping in modern society. In order to ensure appraisal decisions mindful of history in the long run, rather than of legal and administrative concerns in the short run, a strong coalition of interests will have to again emerge. Nothing short of a revival of the spirit and approach of the Business Historical Society will be truly effective. At its most active stage, the society represented executives, archivists, and historians, all of whom were concerned with the preservation of history. They were convinced that the country and its economy would be well served if future generations understood the formation, development, and influence of the country's economic institutions. This view was hardly characteristic of all businessmen at the time. The fear of access, inclination to destroy, and lack of a general sense of history existed then as it does now.[32] But a sufficient number of business executives of stature and influence saw the importance of the work of the Business Historical Society and worked toward achieving its goals. Significant numbers of historians at important universities were actively engaged in the use of what records were made available. Archivists, curators, and librarians at relevant institutions were willing to support the society, too. Thus, a strong coalition of interests of executives, historians, and archivists contributed to a successful program in the 1920s. Any large-scale analysis of modern corporate records and structure will require the cooperation of all interests represented in that old coalition. Times have changed. Suspicions increase as size and image make corporate organizations seem increasingly remote. Yet there are some hopeful signs. Harold Anderson, of Wells Fargo Bank, has concluded that, "Business archives are coming of age as more and more companies reap the benefits of one of their most useful and inexpensive corporate assets."[33] The recently published history of Delta Air Lines Company, done by professional historians with full access to the corporate records, is also a hopeful sign that interest in history and the historical record within the business community is still present, and in some cases strong.[34] For the appraisal of the corporate record, such a coalition will have to be identified and strengthened in order to provide the environment necessary for the undertaking of major studies of corporate structure and records. Only with the joint consultation of experienced executives, archivists, and historians can meaningful and influential studies of the process and adequacy of documentation of the corporate enterprise be done.

A final concern regards the appraisal process itself. Assuming the completion of abstract studies of structure and other studies on the nature of record keeping, an awareness of the broader influence of business institutions, and a well-organized coalition of interests, what can be said about the nature of the appraisal process? The size of corporate institutions, their traditional remoteness from the research community, their enormous capacity to produce records of varying quality—all of these factors suggest that the question of appraisal is essentially an academic one. Can any meaningful selection be done in a universe of documentation so vast, varied, and restricted? If the nature of the institutions and their structures are thoroughly understood, then, yes, selection can be done. Appraisal requires well-researched frameworks of analysis and must include an understanding of process, institutional structures, models of communication, and the nature and function of records in a modern society. It poses intellectual questions because appraisal problems require analysis on a large and complex scale. When business was small and locally oriented, appraisal problems were small. Now that the structure of the U.S. economy increasingly rests on large multifunctional, multinational corporations, the problem of appraisal has become that much more complex, too. No longer can one simply skim through the records of a company and sift out the important from the unimportant. The appraisal of business records requires considerably more research and analysis. Moreover, as corporate records managers take on the archival function of the modern corporation, the challenge of the appraisal of modern corporate records will not be the actual process of selection, but rather the ability to inject a greater concern for the historical, rather than the administrative and legal, in the formulation of corporate retention policies. Through systematic study, analysis, and debate about what should constitute the historical record of modern corporations, cases for broader retention policies can be made.[35]

There is no simple solution to the appraisal problem; appraisal is an inexhaustible issue. There will be no definitive studies. No simply stated rules are likely to emerge; only studies of specific organizational problems, specific record groups, and specific structural forms will be forthcoming.

The publication and exchange of such studies, a well-reasoned and documented intellectual dialogue based on specific problems, can only lead to a refinement of perspective on the appraisal process. At no time is a perfect appraisal of modern records likely to occur. Over time, through rigorous research based on discussion and reasoned application, the documents of modern business enterprises can be assembled. The value of such ongoing research and discussion will be the improved judgment and focus of archivists in making selections.

The role of archivists with regard to the appraisal of business records is twofold. First, the archival profession at large is in need of better developed studies of structure and environment in relation to U.S. business institutions. Then, on the basis of these studies and, given a sense of the historiographical trends and issues in U.S. business history, archivists can make judicious selection from the universe of documentation. Moreover, with help of interested and influential executives and historians, an archivist may be able to influence the selection processes and procedures within a company. This is an agenda that advocates first, systematic thought and analysis and then action. The challenge that modern business collections pose to archivists requires that intellectual steps be taken before actual selection is done. Through continued research, active and patient dialogue, and carefully thought out selection, the record of modern U.S. businesses can be assembled in a thorough and efficient way.

Notes

1. See Walter M. Whitehill, *Independent Historical Societies* (Boston: The Boston Athenaeum, 1962).

2. See, in particular, American Historical Association, *Annual Reports*, 1895-1905, which included the results of these surveys, and Victor Gondos, Jr., *J. Franklin Jameson and the Birth of the National Archives 1906-1926* (Philadelphia: University of Pennsylvania Press, 1981); see, also, James A. Robertson, *List of Documents in Spanish Archives Relating to the History of the United States . . .* (Washington, D.C.: Carnegie Institution, 1910); Herbert E. Bolton, *Guide to Materials for the History of the United States in the Principal Archive of Mexico* (Washington, D.C.: Carnegie Institution, 1913); Albert B. Faust, *Guide to the Materials for American History in Swiss and Austrian Archives* (Washington, D.C.: Carnegie Institution, 1916).

3. Henrietta Larson, *Guide to Business History* (Cambridge, Mass.: Harvard University Press, 1948), p. 986.

4. See *Bulletin of the Business Historical Society*, particularly issues published between 1926 and 1930.

5. Arthur H. Cole, "Business Manuscripts: A Pressing Problem . . . The Accumulated Development of Unsolved Problems," *Journal of Economic History* 5 (May 1945): 46.

6. Ralph M. Hower, *The Preservation of Business Records* (Boston: Business Historical Society, 1941).

7. Ibid., p. 10.

8. Ibid., pp. 11-17.

9. Cole, "Business Manuscripts," p. 43.

10. Ibid.

11. Ibid., p. 44.

12. Ibid.

13. Ibid.

14. Ibid., pp. 43-46.

15. Ibid., pp. 52-53. See, also, Thomas C. Cochran, "The New York Committee on Business Records," *Journal of Economic History* 5 (May 1945): 60-64.

16. Cole, "Business Manuscripts," p. 57. Reprinted with permission.

17. Henry E. Edmunds, "The Ford Motor Company Archives," *American Archivist* 15 (April 1952): 99-104.

18. Robert W. Lovett, "The Appraisal of Older Business Records," *American Archivist* 15 (April 1952): 231-239.

19. Larry Steck and Francis X. Blouin, Jr., "Hannah Lay and Company: Sampling the Records of a Century of Lumbering in Michigan," *American Archivist* 39 (January 1976): 15-20.

20. Robert Levy, "Inside Industry's Archives," *Dun's Review* 117 (May 1981): 76.

21. The years such programs were created and the creating companies were 1943, Firestone; 1944, INA; 1946, Time, Inc.; 1947, Armstrong Cork; 1949, Alcoa, Lever Brothers, Eastman Kodak; 1950, Texaco; 1951, Ford; 1954, Rockefeller Family; 1955, Sears Roebuck, New York Life Insurance; 1956; Eli Lilly; 1957, Proctor and Gamble; 1958, Bank of America, Coca-Cola; 1961, IBM; 1965, Gulf Oil; 1968, Chicago Board of Trade; 1969, Educational Testing Service; 1970, Walt Disney Productions, Ford Foundation; 1971, International Harvester, Anheuser-Busch; 1973, Corning Glass Works; 1974, Weyerhaeuser, Nationwide Insurance; 1975, Wells Fargo Bank, Chase Manhattan Bank; 1976, Deere & Company, Gerber Products; 1977, Georgia Pacific Company; 1978, Los Angeles Times; 1979, Atlantic Richfield, New York Stock Exchange, J. Walter Thompson. Source: David R. Smith, "An Historical Look at Business Archives." *American Archivist* 45 (Summer 1982): 278.

22. Francis X. Blouin, Jr., "A New Perspective on the Appraisal of Business Records," *American Archivist* 42 (July 1979): 312-320.

23. See the *Federal Register*, a publication of the National Archives and Records Service of the General Services Administration, particularly the periodic pamphlet entitled, *Guide to Record Retention Requirements*.

24. *Douglas Bakken, "Corporate Archives Today," American Archivist* 45 (Summer 1982): 279-286.

25. See Alfred D. Chandler, *The Visible Hand: The Managerial Revolution in America* (Cambridge, Mass.: Belknap Press, 1977), and W. David Lewis and Wesley P. Newton, *Delta: The History of an Airline* (Athens, Ga.: University of Georgia Press, 1979).

26. Alfred D. Chandler, "The Beginnings of 'Big Business' in American Industry," *Business History Review* 33 (Spring 1959): 1-30.

27. Alfred D. Chandler, *Strategy and Structure: Chapters in the History of Industrial Enterprise* (Cambridge, Mass.: M.I.T. Press, 1962).

28. Lance E. Davis and Douglass C. North, *Institutional Change and American Economic Growth* (Cambridge, England: University Press, 1971).

29. JoAnne Yates, "Development of Internal Communication in Business Organizations: Implications for Archival Appraisal," unpublished paper delivered at the meeting of the Society of American Archivists, Boston, 1982. Michael Lutzker, "Max Weber and the Analysis of Modern Bureaucratic Organization: Notes Toward a Theory of Appraisal," *American Archivist* 45(Spring 1982): 119-130.

30. See Theodore R. Schellenberg, *Modern Archives* (Chicago: University of Chicago Press, 1956); Blouin, "A New Perspective."

31. Thomas C. Cochran, *Business in American Life* (New York: McGraw-Hill, 1972).

32. See Ralph M. Hower, "Problems and Opportunities in the Field of Business History," *Bulletin of the Business Historical Society* 15 (April 1941): 17-26.

33. Harold P. Anderson, "Business Archives: A Corporate Asset," *American Archivist* 45 (Summer 1982): 264-266.

34. Lewis and Newton, *Delta.*

35. An interesting example of a study of a specific structural problem with implications for appraisal is H. Thomas Johnson, "Management Accounting in an Early Multidivisional Organization: General Motors in the 1920s," *Business History Review* 52 (Winter 1978): 490-517.

4

Appraisal of Twentieth-Century Congressional Collections

Patricia Aronsson

Twentieth-century congressional collections present archivists with unprecedented challenges.[1] Comprising characteristics of both public records and personal papers, they are difficult to process and are becoming expensive to maintain. Furthermore, dwindling research use raises questions about their value compared to the value of other types of archival collections. These problems, in addition to diminishing staff, space, and financial resources, contribute to the crisis facing archivists who are trying to deal effectively with the collections of recent U.S. senators and representatives.

Congressional collections are hybrids, neither strictly archival nor strictly personal. According to the Society of American Archivists' "Basic Glossary," personal papers are "formed by or around an individual or family" while records represent the "cumulation of a corporate entity."[2] Congressional collections fit both definitions. Most archivists treat the papers of senators or representatives as personal papers, processing them as they would process most manuscript collections. That is, they examine collections at the item level, discard little, and refolder most of the material. Processing such papers with a straight records approach, however, may not be any more appropriate. While an archivist or records manager can easily establish a retention schedule to meet the needs of most same-type, same-size businesses, one schedule is not likely to work for all members of Congress. Each congressional office revolves around a unique personality and the needs of a single state or congressional district. Thus, traditional formulas do not help archivists to make these collections useful.

Congressional collections are more expensive to acquire and maintain than they have ever been. In recent years, the quantity of information accumulated in the personal offices of senators and representatives has increased dramatically. Members of Congress accrue between fifty and one hundred cubic feet of papers per year. Their predecessors of fifty years ago accumulated this quantity over a career of twenty years.[3] Several factors contribute to this proliferation of papers. Constituents write their representatives and senators more often and about more issues than they did in the past. Senators and representatives are called upon to address a greater variety of legislative issues than ever before and, to accommodate these legislative demands, they employ more staff members than did their colleagues of twenty and more years ago. As staff increases, so does the amount of paper produced. Furthermore, legislative employees have become more specialized to meet the more complicated demands made upon senators and representatives. This specialization and the amount of paper produced have increased the time and money needed to evaluate the records and to prepare them for research use. In an effort to avoid being inundated with thousands of boxes of records at one time (when a member retires or is defeated), many repositories send archivists to Washington to arrange for the shipment of small quantities of records periodically throughout the career of the senator or representative. This approach also has drawbacks, however. First, annual or biannual trips to Washington, D.C., are expensive and often result in the acquisition of mundane records. Second, congressional offices frequently request access to records already sent to the repository. Valuable staff time is expended responding to these requests. Considering that congressional collections occupy enormous amounts of shelf space, the maintenance costs of which increase yearly, and require substantial investments of staff time in acquisitions, processing, and servicing, one begins to understand why the question of their value for historical purposes has become so crucial.

Yet the value of these collections as scholarly documents may not justify their expense because, as noted earlier, research use of congressional papers has plummeted in recent years. In 1978, at the Conference of the Research Use and Disposition of Senators' Papers, Robert Warner noted that it would take a researcher ten years to examine every document in an average-size senate collection.[4] Few scholars are able to devote that much time to a single collection. Additionally, the sheer bulk of these collections makes it difficult for a researcher to locate particular pieces of information. To document their studies of Congress, many scholars have turned to other sources, such as the *Congressional Record*, executive-branch documents, published reports and hearings, and other secondary materials. Without doubt, the current condition of most congressional collections discourages research use.

How, then, should archivists approach contemporary congressional collections? It has become apparent that standard archival practices and theories do not accommodate the special problems presented by these collections. Traditionally, in an attempt to maintain what they understand as the integrity of a collection, archivists have retained tremendous quantities of duplicative and historically insignificant information. The concept of provenance discourages archivists from looking at several congressional collections simultaneously and appraising them so that they complement one another. Archivists also often fail to consider how the substantive issues documented in a congressional collection are addressed in other noncongressional collections. Consequently, congressional collections are far larger than they need to be in order to reflect the important issues and activities that they document. Certainly, archivists are bound to respect the integrity of their holdings, but the meaning of integrity must be reevaluated if repositories are going to continue to acquire collections that typically exceed one thousand cubic feet and contain large quantities of nonunique materials. When archivists employ traditional methods in their handling of congressional collections, no one's needs are adequately met. The repository is burdened with an enormous collection, the preparation of which requires years of a processor's time. Researchers are overwhelmed by the volume and often find it difficult to locate information. The donor is disappointed when he learns that the collection will not be available for years and that, even then, it will generate little research interest.

Thus, congressional collections require a new approach, one that addresses the many problems inherent in these collections. Because many of the drawbacks of these collections are a consequence of their size, it follows that the new strategy should focus on ways to shrink these collections. While appraising to winnow the size of collections is not a new archival technique, archivists typically weed out only categories of material that are generally acknowledged to have little historical significance, such as routine housekeeping records, duplicates, and published information.[5]

When appraising congressional collections, archivists should first take into account the fact that several series within a congressional collection are usually duplicated in the collections of all other members of Congress who served during the same time period. All senators and representatives serving simultaneously receive correspondence about the entire spectrum of issues that will come before them on the floor of the House or the Senate. Additionally, to permit them to vote intelligently, all members of Congress must obtain sufficient background information on these issues. Second, archivists should be aware that each of these collections, even though it consists of the records of an office, revolves around a single personality, that of the senator or representative. Finally, archivists should keep in mind that the congressional collection they have acquired is only one of 535 similar collections (the total number of senators and representatives serving at one time). Only by paring down these collections to their unique elements will archivists succeed in making them useful to researchers and manageable for archives.

This appraisal approach requires meticulous background work. Archivists must become as familiar as possible with the U.S. Congress, the individual senator or representative, her office, and the issues important to her home state. Only by thoroughly understanding the context in which the records are created can the archivist be certain of the validity of his appraisal decisions. The ideal time for an archivist to gain these insights is while the senator or representative is still in office. Then the archivist can observe the operation of the congressional office, learn from congressional staff members what issues are of special importance to the member of Congress, and inquire about the value of particular categories of information.

Becoming involved with a congressional collection while it is being created offers the archivist additional benefits. The archivist can work with the congressional office to ensure that it has a viable records-management program. He can take advantage of the support services offered to senators and representatives. For example, the Senate offers micrographics services free of charge to current senators. Both senators and representatives also have access to automated systems that can facilitate the indexing of certain portions of the collection.

Archivists should be careful, though, not to interfere with the creation of records. The archivist's role in Congress is to observe and understand, not to persuade the office to create or store information in ways that facilitate archival use but do not enhance office use.

Every archivist responsible for congressional collections should learn about Congress first hand. Such knowledge enables the archivist to identify the unique characteristics of individual collections. Archivists also find it useful to compare their observations with each other. The following description of congressional office activities and assessment of the records created are based upon the author's experience in four congressional offices.

Understanding the Congressional Office

Senate and House offices all engage in the same three activities: meeting constituent needs, representing the home district's interests in Congress, and legislating national policies.

Senators and representatives serve their constituents in a variety of ways. When home-state residents visit Washington, D.C., Senate and House offices cater to their needs. They provide tickets for tours to the White House and other federal buildings as well as to the Senate and House galleries. Some congressional offices even prepare elaborate tour guides for their constituents. Congressional offices are no less responsive to written requests. They send constituents autographed photographs, flags that have flown over the Capitol, items for charity auctions, and birthday greetings. Most congressional offices have one staff person who devotes at least part of every day to filling constituent requests.

Senate and House offices also meet constituent needs through casework, a term that refers to a congressional office's efforts to help an individual solve a specific problem with a federal or state agency. Essentially, the congressional office serves as the liaison between constituent and agency. Most casework involves problems in getting social-security checks, welfare assistance, veterans' benefits, or travel visas. In a typical case, a constituent writes to his senator or representative seeking help with a problem. The office photocopies the letter and sends it to the appropriate federal or state agency, along with a note or "buck slip" asking the agency to please assist this constituent. Some offices ask the agency to respond directly to the constituent but others prefer to serve as the conduit between the constituent and the agency. In either case, the office writes back to the constituent to say that the senator or representative has intervened on the constituent's behalf and he should hear about the resolution of the problem soon. Casework requires a tremendous amount of paperwork and staff time. Most congressional offices employ between two and five people to handle casework. Some senators and representatives view casework as the most effective way they can serve their constituents.

Congressional casework meets an important need, but it is not one of the fundamental responsibilities of members of Congress. Representing the state's or district's interests in the House or the Senate is a key responsibility, and most members of Congress fulfill this obligation in one of two ways. The first is for the senator or representative to sponsor or at least vote in favor of legislation that benefits his state or certain segments of its population. For example, the elected representatives from Connecticut pay particular attention to legislation that could affect the insurance industry. The second way that senators and representatives represent their state's or district's interests is by helping to channel federal dollars into the state. Often, state and local groups write their senators or representative asking for support and assistance in their efforts to obtain federal funds. Most congressional offices write letters endorsing grant applications from home-state applicants. Some offices review applications and offer to help the groups complete the necessary forms. Others arrange meetings between the applicants and the granting agency or work closely with local agencies to develop fundable project proposals. Congressional offices usually employ at least one individual who works full-time helping state and local agencies (and individuals) compete for federal dollars. This same individual often monitors federal legislation that could affect the state and reports this information to the representative or senator.

While most members of Congress devote considerable energy to serving their home states, they also are responsible for legislating national policies. The U.S. Congress considers legislation pertaining to an incredible range of issues: social, domestic, foreign, trade and manufacturing, regulatory. No one member of Congress could ever become an expert in all the subject areas upon which he must vote. Consequently, senators and representatives employ subject specialists to advise them. The staff of every congressional office includes several people who monitor legislation about to come before the Congress. These staff people prepare background reports and often recommend to their senator or representative how to vote. Legislative staff members attend the numerous hearings held in the Senate and the House, and they assimilate and condense all this information for presentation to their employer. Legislative staff also keep track of how people back home are reacting to particular issues and inform the senator or representative so he can take that information into consideration when voting.

By understanding the major congressional activities—meeting constituent needs, representing the home district's interests, and legislating national policies—archivists acquire the necessary framework for evaluating the records. But archivists also must familiarize themselves with those characteristics that make each office unique. Only then are they equipped to effectively appraise congressional records.

The residents of each state and of every congressional district within it demand different services from their elected officials. For example, West Virginia residents seek congressional assistance to ensure that protection against black lung and other mine-safety legislation is enacted. Consequently, the papers of West Virginia's senators and representatives will reflect these special state concerns. Because their constituents care about these issues, representative elected from this region are more attuned to them than are many of their colleagues, and that sensitivity will be reflected in their papers.

Archivists also must realize that senators and representatives have their own pet interests. The office records probably document these interests as fully as they document those issues of importance to the state. Many members serve on at least one committee that addresses their particular concerns and employ at least one individual who specializes in those subjects. When the senator or representative exhibits a special interest in a subject, her staff members make an extra effort to say abreast of developments in that subject area. In addition, senators and representatives receive a great deal of correspondence regarding their special interests from outside experts as well as from knowledgeable amateurs.

Finally, archivists need to identify the popular causes that surfaced during the senator's or representative's tenure. The files probably contain a tremendous amount of mail on these subjects. If these issues captivated the nation, archivists can be certain that every Senate and House office received identical mail. If a senator or representative is identified with a particular social movement, however, it is reasonable to expect that his mail includes more thoughtful and more sophisticated communications on that subject.

Assessing Congressional Records

While every congressional office generates and stores unique information, most of it can be categorized easily. However, each office is organized a bit differently, and the location within the files of any specific type of record varies. This diversity makes the suggestion of detailed retention and disposition schedules impractical. Instead, this section presents descriptions of and disposition recommendations for the major categories of information found in most congressional offices. The categories are listed in order of descending research potential.

Administrative Assistant's Files

The administrative assistant is the staff director in the senator's or representative's personal office. Typically, this individual is the senior staff person. His responsibilities are diverse and often include monitoring the member's political standing, both locally and nationally, overseeing key legislative issues, and supervising the senator's or representative's staff. The administrative assistant also handles the most sensitive telephone calls and correspondence.

Very often, administrative assistants retain few files. They conduct a lot of their work over the telephone and, because of its sensitive nature, they commit little to paper. The routine responsibilities of the administrative assistant are usually the most fully documented aspects of her job. Other records that often survive include memos between the assistant and the representative or senator, correspondence with the boss's personal friends, personnel files, and legislative research files.

The administrative assistant's files should be preserved in their entirety. This person plays such an important role in the congressional office that his activities should be documented as fully as possible. Although a moderate amount of this material may not merit preservation, the end result of weeding the files does not justify the amount of time this task would require, particularly because this series is likely to be the smallest in the entire collection.

Legislative Assistants' Files

Legislative assistants monitor legislation and advise their senator or representative about all legislation pending before the House or the Senate. The number of legislative assistants in Senate and House offices varies from two to as many as seven per office. Usually, there are fewer legislative assistants in a House office than in a Senate office. Consequently, legislative assistants in the House are less specialized than their Senate counterparts. However, because the issues before Congress are so diverse, every legislative assistant must be responsible for several, unrelated subjects. Legislative assistants are engaged in a variety of activities: they answer some of the mail that comes into the office on the topics for which they are responsible, they monitor all pending legislation in those areas, they meet with lobbyists and constituents who want to discuss issues, and they assist the senator or representative on the Senate or House floor and with all preliminary work for measures the senator or representative sponsors. In some offices, legislative assistants suggest possible legislative initiatives to their bosses, and many are acknowledged experts in at least one of the areas they handle. Legislative assistants comprise the majority of the professional staff in most congressional offices.

The types of files legislative assistants keep depend upon the filing system their office uses. In an office with centralized files, they keep only their research and pending files at their desks; all their correspondence and memos are filed in the office's central files. Many legislative assistants working in offices with centralized filing systems keep a chronological file of their memos as well as copies of their most important correspondence. In offices where staff maintain their own files, legislative assistants typically keep at hand their correspondence and memos, notes of their meetings with lobbyists and other people, notes from the hearings and other committee meetings they attend, copies of speeches they wrote, and their research files. Their files usually reflect both their special interests and the interests of their boss. In most congressional offices, legislative assistants establish their own filing systems. Many of them organize their files by legislative bill number, others organize them by subject, and still others arrange their papers chronologically.

The files of legislative assistants should be kept in their entirety unless the archivist has sufficient time to process them item by item. This is the only series that archivists should consider processing at the item or folder level. These files usually include a great deal of bulky, published material, much of which can be discarded. Archivists should be cautious in discarding material, however; some of the publications may not be available from other sources because they were not distributed widely. Many small organizations produce publications and reports for lobbying purposes, for example. The Library of Congress also prepares reports for congressional offices. These reports are not available elsewhere, and the quality of the work frequently is outstanding. Legislative assistants' files are likely to be the most substantive in a senator's or representative's collection because, unlike the administrative assistant, legislative assistants often keep a paper record of their work. The greatest problems archivists will face with these records is finding them—legislative assistants often take their files with them when they leave the employ of the senator or representative.

Press Files

Press files contain the senator's or representative's speeches, press releases, newsletters, miscellaneous writings, and all the published articles about her. Most press files are arranged in chronological order, with each item filed in a separate folder. Press files provide valuable information about the attitudes and opinions of the senator or representative and should be kept in their entirety. Archivists probably should not refolder this material, however, because of the wealth of information found on the folder labels—title of speech or release, place and date of delivery, and sponsoring organization (if a speech). In at least one congressional office, where the information was placed on the label indicated whether or not the member received an honorarium. All speeches a senator or representative delivered on the House or Senate floor appear in the *Congressional Record*, which is fully indexed. While some archivists may be inclined to discard loose copies of these speeches, they should remember that juxtaposing them with the member's other speeches can facilitate research use.

Project Files

As mentioned earlier in this chapter, senators and representatives work to channel federal money to their home states. The files that document these efforts are usually labeled as projects or grants and projects files. Typically projects files include the entire dossier on each project with which the senator or representative was involved. The file contains a copy of the original application for funds, the application's supporting documentation, correspondence between the applicant and the congressional office, and correspondence between the congressional office and the funding body.

In many congressional offices, projects personnel are left alone to devise their own filing system. Some projects staff develop elaborate systems that allow them to retrieve information from any of a number of reference points, such as county, funding agency, type of grant or loan, date of application. The archivist must solicit from the projects staff a copy of their file guide. Project files provide important information about the state and should be preserved.

Personal Files

More often than not, the label, "personal files," is a misnomer. Few members of Congress keep files of a truly personal nature in their offices. These files are labeled personal because they contain the material that was brought to the attention of the senator or representative. Personal files contain a tremendous amount of information about the senator's or representative's daily activities. Included here are invitations to social and business events, letters between the senator or representative and those VIPs with whom he has become friendly or whom the staff has decided are of sufficient importance to merit personal responses, and records of the senator's or representative's personal meetings.

This file consists mostly of correspondence, invitations, phone and visitor logs, and the senator's or representative's appointment calendars. In many congressional offices, these records are separated from the other records created in the office. Sometimes the personal secretary keeps these files at his desk, and sometimes they are divided among the administrative assistant, the appointments secretary, and the personal secretary. The category, personal files, may include information that has little if any historical value, such as office expense records (the member of Congress is required to personally sign many expense vouchers), invitations that have been rejected, and routine personnel matters.

Invitations require special attention by the archivist because some (those that were accepted) merit preservation while others (those that were rejected) do not. Accepted invitations reveal the activities of an individual member of Congress and also may help a researcher identify categories of social events attended by high-level federal officials. Many archivists and historians argue that rejected invitations are of value, too, because they identify those organizations that a member of Congress did not think were of sufficient importance to warrant his support. Most representatives and senators cannot possibly accept all of the invitations they receive, and their reasons for turning down any given invitation would be almost impossible to determine. Researchers who want to study rejected invitations can identify these invitations by going through the computerized indexes of the office's correspondence.

The senator's or representative's personal files are valuable for the insights they provide about the member's activities while an elected official. The personal files reflect the senator's or representative's life style and ways of interacting with cohorts, and they contribute to a researcher's understanding of the senator or representative as a person.

Administrative Files

The office's internal files are known as administrative files. Archivists often overlook these files, which include file keys, support files for the automated records, and staff lists.

Almost every congressional office prepares some type of key to its files, but few include this key with records sent to the archives. As the files change and new keys are prepared, some offices destroy the earlier file codes. Without adequate file codes, archivists spend a great deal of time trying to decipher the filing system. When unable to do so, they often rearrange the files into chronological or alphabetical order. Reorganizing records is a time-consuming process and can compromise the integrity of the collection. Instead of waiting until the collection arrives at the repository to see if the file system can be easily understood, the archivist should visit the congressional office as early in the member's career as possible and establish a working relationship with the office manager. The archivist should request that one copy of each successive file code be sent to the repository along with an explanation of the changes in the code.

Archivists also face a serious problem if the office does not preserve its compendium of computerized form letters. The computer tapes, both Senate and House, contain only indexing information; they do not include the texts of the letters. Some congressional offices discard the master copies of their form letters once the language becomes outdated. If they do this, the value of the computer indexes diminishes because the indexes identify form letters solely by their identification numbers (see appendix 4A). Without the actual texts, researchers will be unable to reconstruct the content of the correspondence. As early as possible, archivists should inquire about the office's policy toward outdated form letters and, if necessary, should persuade the office to retain a permanent master file of such letters.

A list of all former and current staff members is another valuable research tool. With such a list, researchers can determine authorship for every initialed document. If a researcher knows who wrote a document and the position held by that person in the office, he is better able to reconstruct the hierarchy of decision making in a congressional office. Archivists or researchers can, at any time, generate a staff list by going through the salary reports published by both houses of Congress, but it is easier for congressional offices to prepare such a list because they can engage the help of the administrative officers of Congress. Furthermore, many congressional office managers would find a list of this type useful for various administrative purposes.

Issue Mail

Issue mail presents archivists with some difficult decisions. Citizens from all over the country write to their elected officials about every conceivable topic. And, while each congressional collection should not have to document the universe of issues concerning the U.S. people, it should reflect those issues that were important to the senator or representative and his staff. Typically, congressional offices pay little attention to letters about issues with which the senator or representative is not especially concerned. The office answers such letters with form responses that either present the member's position on that issue or simply thank the correspondents for sharing their views. On the other hand, letters about the senator's or representative's special interests often provoke an individualized response prepared by the legislative assistant responsible for that subject area. Both these categories of mail are often integrated in the files. While it is relatively simple for archivists to use the computer indexes to separate the two catego- ries, they must first identify what issues fit into which category. To do so, archivists must study the career of the particular senator or representative and talk to her staff, bearing in mind, though, that the interests of members of Congress change over time. Archivists should make an effort to identify those issues with which the member used to be involved by talking to long-time staff members as well as to former employees and by looking through the speech and press-release files.

Issue mail, because of its volume and repetitiveness, lends itself to sampling. Offices that use automated systems prepare most of their issue mail with the help of a computer. If archivists become involved with a collection while the member of Congress is still in office, they can elicit the help of either the Senate computer center or the vendor used by the House office in preparing the computer programs needed to generate a statistically valid sample. The decision about whether to sample depends on two factors. First, archivists must recognize that, in generating a sample, they are com- mitting the repository to preserving material it would not otherwise retain— a sample of routine correspondence about issues not important to the principal of the collection. Second, the repository must have sufficient space to store this material and sufficient personnel to service it. Once archivists decide to sample, they must determine the purpose of that sample; for example, to document the range of interests expressed by constituents or to show how interest in a particular issue corresponds to geographical region.

Political Files

Information about the senator's or representative's campaigns for reelection as well as information about other home-state political races are included in political files. Federal regulations mandate the separation of personal staff and campaign staffs. Consequently, many congressional offices do not even store campaign records in Washington. Instead, they scatter these files among the campaign manager's home or office, the candidate's home, and the homes of various campaign workers. Archivists will have to hunt for the

background information candidates used in formulating their position statements as well as for campaign literature. Archivists should not routinely
discard the information a senator or representative retains about someone
else's political races; the senator or representative may have viewed this
person as a possible future opponent or may have borrowed the person's
rhetoric or format of his campaign literature.

Whenever possible, political files should be preserved. These files provide useful grist for scholars of various disciplines, but they may contain
confidential information. Unless the archivist convinces the donor that the
confidentiality of the political files will be respected, this material may well
be destroyed before it ever reaches an archives.

Casework Files

Casework files are one of the more voluminous categories of information
found in a senator's or representative's office. And, although the staff
devotes a tremendous amount of time to helping constituents with their
personal problems, the historical significance of this category is minimal.
Every congressional office handles large quantities of casework, much of it
identical to that answered by other congressional offices. Researchers need
to know that casework consumed much congressional staff time, but they
probably have little use for the actual letters. Some letters are poignant and
reveal the agonies people experience, but researchers can more efficiently
identify the problems of the U.S. people from other archival records, such as
the collections of social welfare agencies. Researchers cannot expect congressional collections to document the whole of the U.S. experience.
Because this material is bulky and can be found in other sources, the
archivist should consider recommending to the congressional office staff
that they schedule casework for periodic destruction. Archivists should be
aware, though, that many constitutents send members of Congress important original documents, such as birth certificates and military discharge
papers, and they should urge the congressional office to return these documents to the constituents as soon after receiving them as possible.

Some casework should be preserved. Certain problems are unique to a
specific geographical region (such as the problem of black-lung disease in
West Virginia), and the corresponding casework reflects a special characteristic of that region. Casework also should be preserved when a senator or
representative is particularly interested in an issue that generated case mail,
such as the refugee problem (immigration casework) or veterans' affairs.

Casework contains little substantive information, but many researchers
relish its anecdotal value. To accommodate them, archivists may choose to
retain a small sample of the case files. Archivists who decide to keep case-

work, however, must develop access policies that protect the privacy of the individuals who wrote to their senator or representative for help.

Newsclippings Files

Newsclippings can be found in all congressional offices. Many senators and representatives subscribe to clipping services and most accumulate huge quantities of clippings, often gluing them into oversized scrapbooks. Many congressional offices keep multiple copies of identical articles, one for each time it appeared in a local paper. Staff members often believe that newspaper and magazine articles are the essence of history, and they make special efforts to preserve this material.

An archivist's decision about whether to keep a clippings file should reflect the resources of his repository. Some archives index all the home-state newspapers and would have no need for a senator's or representative's clippings file. Others would view these files as a valuable addition to their resources. If an archivist decides to keep the clippings, she may want to request that the congressional office have them microfilmed and ship only the film to the archives.

An alternative approach, and one that works well in some congressional offices, is for the office itself to selectively preserve clippings. Senator Russell Long's press assistant retains one copy of every published article about Senator Long. She keeps only one copy of wire-service stories. After collecting an entire day's clippings, she photocopies them all and puts one photocopy aside for the archives. Additional copies of these articles are distributed to the senator and his staff. Preparing the one archival copy requires very little extra work on her part and satisfies the office's desire to keep all clippings about the senator. The clippings are then filed in one place, in chronological order, and in good physical condition.

Photography Files

Photographs, like newsclippings, sometimes present more problems than they seem to be worth. Senators and representatives pose for photographs with almost every tour group from their home state, and their offices often keep file copies. Only the most organized offices label these photographs; others simply file them. The photographs' historical value is negligible, particularly when they are not identified. However, even the identified group shots reveal little information.

Some photographs, though, may be historically significant—candid shots of the member's official travels, her personal photographs, and shots of the senator or representative in action. Such photographs are often difficult to locate, however. Those sent in by friends and admirers may be filed in the office's main filing system. The archivist must decide how much time to spend searching for them, keeping in mind that public officials are accustomed to being photographed and even the most casual shot may be totally contrived. Although photographs found in congressional collections may not be intrinsically valuable, they can enhance exhibits and are useful as illustrations in publications. Archivists must carefully evaluate their repositories' interest in photographs before deciding whether to keep them.

Academy Files

Senators and representatives are offered the opportunity to recommend candidates to all U.S. military academies, and students from all over the state write their elected officials seeking such recommendations. The academy files in a congressional office typically include correspondence with the applicant as well as the applicant's references and academic history. Some members of Congress stay in touch with the candidates they recommend, others do not. Most archivists agree that the files of the rejected applicants offer little information of interest to researchers. There is, though, disagreement about the value of the files of the accepted applicants. Some archivists contend that these files reveal data about political patronage or, because many illustrative U.S. citizens have attended military academies, may contain information about future national leaders. It is doubtful, however, that a researcher would make a special trip to look at Senator X's academy files. Furthermore, these files are not the only source of this information. The academies themselves maintain files on all their students. Unless a congressional office closely follows the careers of the students the member recommended, these files need not be preserved.

Requests Files

Most congressional offices keep a separate file containing all routine requests for items such as photographs of the senator or representative, his biographical sketch, flags flown over the Capitol, and tickets for White House tours. These files contain no historically valuable information and can be discarded.

Archival Theory and Practice

The size and the value of twentieth-century congressional collections pose, as noted earlier, serious problems for archives and archivists. Whether their value merits the storage space and staff time their size requires is question-able. Traditional archival practices have led to a dilemma: repositories must either stop acquiring such collections or continue to devote inordinate and growing amounts of space and labor to their care. Strategies that permit archivists to appraise (weed) these collections at some level of detail between that of the collection and the item must be developed. The preceding part of this chapter provided some practical guidelines for embarking upon such a strategy. It offered a sufficiently detailed description of congres-sional offices to permit an interested archivist to develop an appraisal pro-gram. It emphasized that an essential part of that program is early and active interaction with a functioning office.

Archivists should be aware, however, that they will encounter special problems when they accept responsibility for the records of a sitting member of Congress. For example, as mentioned at the beginning of this chapter, the originating office may require access to the materials that have been sent to the archives. These demands may represent one more burden to an already overworked reference staff. Also, many members of Congress will want to seal from research use those portions of their collections that are sent to the repository while the office is still functioning. The archives will have to devote an enormous amount of stack space to a collection that may be sealed from researchers for several years. Finally, because the archivist who joins the staff of a member of Congress represents both the donor and the repository, she may face conflicting interests. Occasionally, a member of Congress or his staff may urge the archivist to destroy records that they deem embarrassing or too sensitive for inclusion in the member's archival collec-tion. As the donor's representative, then, the archivist may find himself negotiating with the repository for unreasonably harsh restrictions. Without question, the demands placed upon a congressional archivist can be trying.

Archivists must recognize that few congressional staff members devote much attention to the future life of the records they create. To ensure the best possible archival collection, though, archivists need the assistance of the staff. When seeking such help, however, they must remain aware that they are treading on shaky ground. While archivists want to guide the shaping of the records so that the files will be useful in the future, they should avoid actually creating records. *Respect du fonds* is not dead: archivists must remember that their needs concerning these records take second place to the use that the office makes of these files. Furthermore, archivists should avoid making staff members overly self-conscious about the records they are creating. An archivist's early involvement with congressional collections can contribute significantly to the final shape of the collection, but these collec-tions must be allowed to develop on their own without too much interfer-ence from the archivist.

The active, interventionist, and differentially selective approach to acquiring and appraising congression collections takes archivists far from some of their most treasured concepts and practices. Maximizing research potential, a value that underlies most archival thinking and practice, is the explicit goal of this approach. Here the dilemma posed by congressional collections becomes clear. From an administrator's perspective, an institution's sparce resources should be allocated to those collections or activities that offer the greatest promise of payoff, in terms of likely use or research value. Collections never acquired offer no research potential. Immense, rich collections that are poorly organized and badly documented are of marginal research value. With a congressional collection, however, its size alone seriously minimizes its research value, regardless of how well-organized or described that collection may be. Archivists must consider the ramifications this bulk will have if they apply standard appraisal methods when approaching congressional collections.

If, however, all archivists were to adopt the perspective outlined in this chapter, another serious problem would quickly surface. The net result would be large numbers of atomistic collections that document only individual congressional offices. This possibility poses questions that the archival profession's thinkers need to address. How can other, sizable institutions be properly documented (at least through this congressional lens) if the focus of each collection is the individual occupant of the office? Can the responsibilities of documenting a larger universe be met without overburdening archival repositories and their patrons? If so, how? And what concepts and principles can be called upon to guide archivists in their appraisals of congressional collections?

These questions are heady and cannot be answered easily. Two different but not mutually exclusive approaches might be explored. First, archivists might reconsider the definition of congressional collections. Second, they might think about creating new institutional alliances. Both ideas, along with their implications for usual archival standards and practices, are explored in the remainder of this chapter.

Redefining Congressional Collections

Archivists need to consider reexamining the definition of congressional collections. The profession has always accepted that the papers of each representative and senator represents an entity, an entire collection. This may be inappropriate. All members of a state's delegation work on the same problems, therefore, their case loads are similar, the projects for which they intervene may overlap, and quite often they discuss the same state issues.

Perhaps archivists should redefine the collection to be the papers of all members of a state's congressional delegation, with the papers of each senator and representative forming a separate subgroup. By pulling together the papers of the entire delegation, archivists could weed out greater quantities from each collection than would otherwise be feasible. Furthermore, the collection of a short-term member of Congress could be greatly enhanced by juxtaposing it with the papers of her more experienced colleagues.

Focusing on the delegation rather than the individual permits archivists to critically evaluate whether the papers of every member of Congress need to be preserved. As long as archivists evaluate collections individually and in isolation, they will continue to justify the acquisition of each member's papers, because each collection documents aspects of the congressional experience. But if archivists appraise each collection as if it were part of a larger whole, they may decide that some collections contribute little, if any, new information.

Redefining congressional collections allows archivists increased flexibility in appraisal and opens the door to an efficient way of coping with the mass of papers received from the offices of U.S. senators and representatives. Although this approach seems to wreak havoc with the archival notion of provenance, perhaps archivists interpret that concept too narrowly. Twentieth-century congressional collections are a new breed of archival material. The old guidelines may no longer apply.

Creating Institutional Alliances

Archivists also need to think about creating new institutional alliances. Cooperation among archivists within a given region could greatly facilitate the handling of congressional collections. Within a region, each repository might document fully one or more routine congressional activity, such as casework or popular legislative issues. Then other repositories within that region could discard those series with the confidence that researchers could still learn about those aspects of congressional life. No one repository would have to bear the burden of documenting the entire range of activities.For example, one repository in New England could document social-security casework; another might collect immigration casework; and yet another could retain all correspondence regarding balancing the federal budget. Under an arrangement such as this, every repository would be free to appraise, organize, and describe the remaining portions of its congressional collections in whatever manner it desired. Those series that the repository agreed to preserve as its regional obligation, however, would have to be appraised and organized in a manner agreed upon by all members of the network. Ideally, this approach would encourage repositories to reduce significantly the size of their congressional collections so that they reflect the essence of the individual senator or representative and his office.

This approach to congressional collections is not without problems. It will require archivists to become experts in the activities they contract to document. Researchers will have to travel as much as a few hundred miles if they are interested in studying the entire scope of congressional activities. Archivists will need to develop suitable mechanisms for working cooperatively. And members of Congress might resist the idea that portions of their collections will become part of a network of similar collections. None of these problems, though, is insurmountable.

Researchers already travel around the country in their efforts to document congressional activities. With a regional approach, they would know where to visit to study particular aspects of Congress and, even more important, they could be confident of finding those aspects well-documented. Congressional scholars would accrue an additional benefit in that they would be able to fully document the range of congressional activities within each of several regions of the United States.

A less direct, but nonetheless important benefit to researchers would be realized if some of the more sophisticated archival repositories would agree once again to collect congressional papers. Recently, several repositories have rejected these collections because of their size and their marginal research value. By working together with other repositories, these institutions could drastically reduce the size of their congressional collections without sacrificing any unique information. Without doubt, researchers are best served when the collections they study are surrounded by complementary materials, both primary and secondary sources. Increasingly, members of Congress donate their papers to small, out-of-the-way repositories. Often, those are the only institutions that will accept the collection. By developing a plan that encourages repositories to keep only portions of a congressional collection, large research centers might once again be willing to collect in this area.

Archivists may be reluctant to embark upon a program of cooperative appraisal of congressional collections for several reasons. Traditionally, archives have had difficulty working together. Also, cooperative ventures often require repositories to shoulder additional financial and administrative burdens. A cooperative approach to congressional collections, however, will save each repository shelf space and processing time.[6] After the initial organizing effort, the only additional administrative activity required will be keeping the network's steering or guidance committee active. Cooperative appraisal of congressional collections will, in the long run, free up staff time, shelf space, and administrative dollars, all of which are scarce in most repositories. Finally, because few repositories currently systematically appraise their congressional collections, most of them would derive great benefits by working with other institutions in this endeavor.

One other stumbling block may be that the members of Congress whose papers are to be collected may hesitate to donate their papers to institutions that are involved in a cooperative venture such as the one proposed. Most senators and representatives donate their papers to archives because they want their careers to be well-documented and because they want researchers to use their papers. Once they understand the difficulties researchers encounter in using congressional collections that have been processed in the traditional manner, however, it seems likely that most members of Congress will support a cooperative approach.

The archival profession must do a great deal of preliminary work before initiating a regional approach to congressional collections. Many questions must be answered. For example, how should the regions be formed? What should be the criteria for joining this network? Is a professed interest in congressional collections sufficient, or must member institutions be actively involved in soliciting congressional collections? Should the network be limited to repositories that meet certain standards? If so, who should develop these standards and what should they be? How will the network operate? At least in its early stages, the network will need a coordinator. Who will select this individual, and who will fund the position? Should the Society of American Archivists (SAA) bear any or all of these responsibilities? If not SAA, then who? All of these questions must be addressed before archivists initiate a cooperative approach to congressional collections.

Conclusion

This chapter has offered some guidelines that may help archivists cope with twentieth-century congressional collections. In addition, it has suggested some new ways to think about these collections. The archival profession must now begin to ask the necessary questions about and to chart the course for the future handling of congressional collections. A new approach is necessary if archivists are to successfully meet the challenges of tomorrow's congressional collections.

Notes

1. Throughout this chapter, the term congressional collections is used to describe the papers created and accumulated in the offices of U.S. senators and members of the U.S. House of Representatives. Committee records and the records of the administrative offices of Congress are ex-

cluded from this discussion because they are defined as federal records and are sent to the National Archives rather than to other types of repositories. For a full discussion of the distinctions between these three categories of congressional information, see Patricia Aronsson, "Congressional Records as Archival Sources," *Government Publications Review* 8A (1981): 295-302.

2. Frank B. Evans et al., "A Basic Glossary for Archivists, Manuscript Curators, and Records Managers," *The American Archivist* 37 (July 1974): 149.

3. At the Library of Congress Manuscript Division, the collection of Emanuel Celler, who served in Congress from 1923 to 1973, is approximately 271 feet, while the collection of Edward Brooke, who served in the Senate from 1967-1979, exceeds 2,000 feet.

4. *Proceedings of the Conference on the Research Use and Disposition of Senators' Papers*, ed. Richard A. Baker, Sept.14-15, 1978, Washington, D.C., p. 172.

5. Theodore R. Schellenberg, *Modern Archives: Principles and Techniques* (Chicago: University of Chicago Press, 1956).

6. Archivists from five repositories in New Hampshire have established an informal network for managing congressional collections. The thrust of their effort is to provide advice to congressional offices.

Appendix 4A:
Automated Systems
in Congress

Cognizant of the problems senators and representatives face in responding to their mail, both the Senate and the House of Representatives have devised systems to help members cope with their correspondence. The U.S. Senate operates a computer center that offers senators a choice of automated systems. The House allocates a certain dollar amount to each representative so he can select an automated system from any vendor he chooses.

Most senators subscribe to Correspondence Management System (CMS), an automated indexing and word-processing system. To use the word-processing capabilities, the senator's office prepares standard responses to the letters it receives or expects to receive. Each response is entered into the computer and assigned a unique number. Then, every time that particular response, or item, can be used to answer a letter, the responsible member of the senator's staff completes a worksheet that says, essentially, send response (item) number x to this name at this address. The computer calls up that response and prints it in the form of a letter with the correct date and proper salutation. CMS has the capacity to store individual paragraphs as well as entire letters. Staff members can identify the responses already stored in the computer by consulting the office's CMS library. The library is a compilation of all the items, both current and outdated, that the office stores, or has stored, on the computer.

CMS also indexes correspondence. Every letter answered by a computer-generated response is assigned several identifiers: document number, constituent's name and address, staff member's initials, type of document, and subject of letter, which consists of a two-word code and item numbers. The computer can sort the correspondence stored in it according to any of these identifiers and will print hard-copy lists for the office's use. This capability precludes the need for the office to maintain cross-reference files, such as a chronological file or an alphabetical file. Only computer-generated responses, however, are automatically included in the indexes. In order to include manually prepared letters, the senator's office must complete data-entry forms and enter the information on these forms into the computer. The information entered is essentially the same information that is automatically entered for computer-generated correspondence. As with the automated correspondence, the computer assigns a document number to the letters entered through data. The document number is a unique ten-digit number, such as 2234351125, the elements of which are:

2   Last digit of calendar year

234   Julian date (234th day of the year)

35   Identifying number for staff member who inputs information into computer

1   Type of letter (1=single letter; 2=data entry; 3=group letter; 0=casework)

125   Daily count for this particular computer operator

The information input into CMS can be sorted in a number of different ways. For example, one can get a list of all the letters answered by one aide or a list of all the letters about the same subject, sorted by county. Archivists should note, though, that the computer tapes needed to create these indexes may be duplicated for use outside the Senate only if the senator has obtained special permission from the Senate Committee on Rules and Administration.

In addition to CMS, the Senate offers senators the IBM System 6, which is basically a word processor with limited indexing capabilities. Most of the offices that do not subscribe to CMS use System 6. Because System 6 cannot accommodate as many entries as CMS, only senators from the smaller states use it.

In the House of Representatives, members may use any automated system they choose. Most offices use one of three on-line systems that have been developed specifically to meet congressional needs. They are: Dialcom, Datatel Mini-Computers (DMC), and Lewis Systems. The three do not differ considerably from one another. Lewis, the newest, provides higher-speed access than do the other two, which are almost identical to each other. All three systems bear striking resemblance to the Senate's CMS, and so they are not described in detail here.

5

Appraisal of Literary Manuscripts

Philip N. Cronenwett

The collection of manuscripts, particularly literary manuscripts, by institutions is a relatively new phenomenon. It has only been in the past one hundred years that manuscripts have been acquired on a systematic basis. The Library of Congress, for example, did not open its Department of Manuscripts and begin to seek papers in a formal manner until 1897. Not until the 1920s did academic institutions actively pursue the manuscripts as well as the publications of poets, novelists, playwrights, and critics.

The appraisal of literary papers is an even more recent phenomenon. While other forms of records have been appraised critically for many years, little work has been done on literary papers. There are several reasons for this. First, as already noted, collecting literary papers is a relatively new pursuit. Second, many writers are greatly venerated or idolized, and it is considered wrong—if not sacrilegious—to discard anything connected with the writers. Third, the composition of literary collections makes appraisal difficult. Richard Eberhart, in the preface to a volume of his collected prose, noted, "It is still a mystery how and why writers become what they are."[1] Other mysteries, at least to some, are what constitutes the papers of an author and how that body of papers should be approached for the purpose of an appraisal.

The Problem of Literary Manuscripts

Shortly after interest in collecting manuscripts developed, the boom years of the great collectors and collections occurred. Nearly every college and university acquired literary manuscripts, either by gift or purchase. The habit of acquiring small bits or large chunks of the papers of an author persists to this day. Often the very heart of a writer's work has been sundered and is shared by cannibals in the guise of manuscript curators throughout the country or the world. For example, some ninety institutions report Robert Frost holdings in *American Literary Manuscripts*.[2] Of these, at least ten libraries have a significant body of his papers. Fragmentation of collections poses a serious problem for both users and the curators who must make serious and, at least in theory, permanent decisions regarding the appraisal of institutional holdings. If they do not have the complete body of papers present, curators must make appraisal judgments in the dark.

Fragmentation of collections is so common that it is often surprising to find an author's papers in a single location. It is also surprising when the author's papers arrive at the institution from a single source or at one time. When it becomes known that an institution is collecting an author, offers from dealers begin to arrive, and donations often follow. If an institution has the time and resources, it can acquire much of the material that is or will become available. Collections built in such a piecemeal manner are not any easier to appraise than partial collections. Much time and effort, not to mention cold cash, must be spent on an "artificial" or aggregate collection before it is ready for appraisal.

What has come to be known as a "natural" collection is often difficult to find. The 1969 revisions in the income-tax laws have made the acquisition of an entire corpus of literary papers a less-than-common occurrence at institutions. Few if any writers present their papers during their lifetimes because they can no longer legitimately deduct the value of the papers as a gift to an institution. Materials arrive at a repository in small increments and almost invariably as deposits. They remain in the storage area of the repository until the creator dies and the estate can benefit from the bequest. Even if the tax laws are changed to once again benefit the creator/donor, fragmentation is likely to continue. Prior to the 1969 tax-law revisions, writers gave only as much as they could legitimately write off on their taxes in a given year. This meant that, in many cases, collections were divided artifically, rather than on the basis of similar materials being given at one time. Another equally serious problem resulting from such fragmentation was the disruption of the chronological development of a collection.

An institution's rationale for collecting can also cause problems. Is the institution collecting the papers for research value, for publicity value, or for autographic value? The answer to this crucial question will determine how a body of papers, whether artificial or natural, is treated. If papers are collected for publicity value, items of little research value might be retained simply because they would make good exhibits or a splash in the media. If papers are collected for their autographic value, correspondence that might otherwise be discarded would be retained. If papers are collected for research value, other determinants, to be discussed in the next section of this chapter, must be considered in their appraisal.

The question of value, whether intrinsic or extrinsic, is often raised when an institution is considering what to retain in and what to remove from a body of papers. In the case of most collections, the actual cash value of the material is of minor importance. For instance, if a decision is made to shred several dozen linear feet of university or business records, the result is scrap paper for a recycling dealer. If, however, several loose envelopes from a literary collection are considered expendable, the institution may need to enlist the aid of a manuscript dealer in disposing of the material. Two examples, both from recent dealers' catalogs, provide explanation. A wrapper signed by Rupert Brooke was offered for nearly a hundred dollars, while a book mailing bag addressed by Robert Frost was offered for half again as much.[3] Awareness of the monetary value of what is being removed from a collection of literary papers is a necessity and, yet, that value must not influence appraisal decisions.

Another difficulty is that there is little or no literature in the field that treats the collecting, accessioning, appraisal, or disposition of literary papers. What little discussion exists is to be found as an adjunct to textual studies produced by literary critics or literary historians. Both the critics and the historians, of course, approach the problem differently than a curator would. There is no standard or norm by which curators can judge the rightness of their appraisal decisions; they have neither precedents nor resources upon which to draw. It is difficult to determine what colleagues are doing in the same situation. Does one retain galley proofs? Should these proofs be turned over to the rare-book librarian?

For that matter, who is responsible for literary manuscripts? In a number of institutions, the curatorial care of literary papers rests with the rare-book librarian rather than with the curator of manuscripts or an archivist. Yet the rare-book librarian views the gray area of appraisal differently than archivists view it. Appraisal does not even mean the same thing to that person as it does to an archivist or a manuscript curator. Unfortunately, many archivists and manuscript curators consider the care of literary papers an onus rather than a challenge and, therefore, are quite willing to pass the burden on to a rare-book librarian. This is unfortunate because the rare-book librarian may be well aware of the distinctions between the various printings of a text but may be less aware of the problems relating to the manuscript of that text. The question of jurisdiction, then, must be considered carefully.

When working with literary papers, a particularly useful tool is the collection-development policy. Simply stated, the policy details the time span, language restraints, geographical bounds, and other parts of the framework upon which a collection is built. The policy can be as brief as the Hoover Institution Archives' half-page statement or as detailed as the two-page statement done for Stanford's Manuscript Collection.[4] Some policies also detail quantity and level of research and list programs that the collection or collections support. Whether they are called collection-development policies, policy statements, or something similar is of no importance. The act of creating a policy forces the curator to rethink the institutional program for and commitment to a literary collection. This allows the curator to determine what is of importance and value to a collection and, therefore, to make sounder decisions during the appraisal process.

The Content of a Collection

Collections of literary papers vary tremendously in quantity, quality, and content. Content alone presents certain interesting challenges. The papers of a writer of fiction will differ from those of a writer of nonfiction, and the papers of a poet may vary greatly from those of a dramatist. Yet, there are, in most cases, similar types of material in each collection. In this section of the chapter, the types of materials found in differing collections will be discussed, and suggestions as to disposition and retention will be given. At the same time, an attempt will be made to find common points among the several types of literary papers.

One of the largest and often the most important group of materials in the collection of an author is the manuscripts of the author's work. These can begin as ideas written in notebooks or on scraps of paper. The early, rough notes of a work are particularly important evidence of the creative process. The germ of a scene for a play or a line for a poem may appear on any sort of paper, from the back of an envelope to a leaf in a notebook of fine paper bound in leather. Robert Frost's notebooks, for example, show how he jotted down ideas and then returned to them years later to rethink, reshape, and rework the ideas into poems. Notebooks or other forms of early trial work are an important source of information on the development of a writer and the writer's work and must be treated with great care.

Variant drafts of a work are almost always found in an author's papers. In some cases, multiple copies of drafts are found. One of the most vexing problems in dealing with literary manuscripts is determining the order of a series of drafts. This can be of great importance. The decision regarding which drafts should be removed from a collection and which should remain cannot be made until the order of the drafts has been determined. In some cases, only the first draft, and perhaps, one middle draft as well as the final draft are necessary to a collection. In other cases, the retention of the original copy of all drafts may be of importance to researchers. In an interview several years ago, Richard Eberhart noted that it was important to him to be able to see all his drafts when he worked on revisions.[5] If it is important to the writer, it may also be important to the researcher.

Whether all copies of a draft found in the collection are retained depends on whether the copies are marked. If an original with annotations and emendations is accompanied by several unmarked carbons or electrostatic copies, it is clear that these copies are redundant and should be removed from the collection. A problem arises, however, when an unmarked original has an emended carbon. For use in exhibitions and the like, the original may be important. For research, the marked carbon is much more important. In the end, decisions regarding retention of manuscripts drafts and their copies depend on the importance of the author, the complexity of the text, and the importance of the text both to the corpus of the author's work and to literature in general.

Galley proofs, because of size and shape, are another problem. Whether copies of galleys and/or page proofs should be retained is a disputed topic. Does one keep a full set of proofs? Or should a proof be retained only if the author had marked a significant change or emendation on the proof? The retention of galleys simply because they are galleys does not seem to be worth the storage space and processing time they would require. Perhaps the rare-book librarian would like to have the proofs for the book collection? On the other hand, a corrected galley or page proof is extremely important to the student or scholar, so proofs with emendations must be retained. Corrected proofs should be studied carefully to ensure that an editor's corrections of misspellings are not confused with significant changes by the author. The intermediate step between manuscript and published work is a bulky, often unwieldy, mass of paper that demands careful scrutiny before a decision on retention is made.

One other type of manuscript, the marked copy of a published work, requires consideration at this point. Changes made by an author after publication are of great interest to the student and scholar. Kenneth Roberts was notorious for making corrections in the texts of his historical novels so that the facts used in his fiction were accurate. His novel *Arundel* (1930) ran through a number of editions and nearly twenty printings. In his copies of each of the printings are numerous changes, all in fact rather than in style.[6] It was from a corrected text that the next printing of a novel was taken. While Roberts was interested in changing the content of his work, other writers have been concerned with changing their style. Frost's copy of the November 1957 issue of *Atlantic Monthly* shows a number of important changes in both the substances and style of his poem "Kitty Hawk." The retention of a printed copy of a work that has been annotated or emended by the author can be of great consequence in the history of the text.

An important adjunct to the manuscripts and other materials relating to a text are the writer's research materials. Many authors, whether writing fiction or nonfiction, amass quantities of materials that relate to the subject at hand. These materials range from copies of books and articles to original documents, artwork, and photographs. Much of this material can be deleted from the author's papers with little or no loss to the integrity of the collection. If the writer is working with nonfiction, the important sources should be noted and acknowledged in the work. If the writer is working in fiction, one needs to be somewhat more judicious in removing research materials from the collection. It may not be easy to identify the source of information in or inspiration for creative writing. Material that was clearly the basis of a creative work is best left in the collection as a part of the resources relating to the text.

A subsidiary area of concern is that of original source material found in the collection. This is a particular concern in the case of papers of authors of nonfiction or historical fiction. Kenneth Roberts, for example, was a meticulous and tireless researcher who spent great amounts of time and money tracking down the books and manuscripts he used in the preparation of his novels. When a collection contains such original material used for research by the writer, it is the usual practice to remove the important documents or manuscripts and treat them as a separate body of papers. There should, of course, be an indication on the cataloging record and in the guide to the papers that the materials are in another body of papers. An important manuscript or series of manuscripts should not be buried within another body of papers simply to preserve what is, at best, an artificial provenance.

Frequently, one of the largest segments, if not *the* largest segment, of a literary collection is correspondence. Correspondence can be conveniently divided into three broad groups: with editor and publisher, with other writers, and with fans. Correspondence with an editor and publisher is an important source of information regarding the writer's creative process, timing, strengths, and limitations. The interplay between writer and editor is important and, if documented in correspondence, can help the researcher better understand the subject. Frost's correspondence with Henry Holt and Company and the several editors with whom he worked shows the evolution of a young poet dealing with a major publisher to a major literary figure dealing almost at will with his publisher. Although this correspondence is not of critical importance, it is important enough to be retained in a collection.

The second group, correspondence with other writers, also illuminates the writer's career. Changes in the relationship between two writers, as careers develop and situations change, are documented in their letters. A good example is the correspondence between Frost and Edward Thomas, the English poet who died during World War I. Their close relationship and its ups and down are carefully delineated in their correspondence. Another example is that of the literary correspondence of Richard Eberhart. Now spanning more than fifty years and contained in over a hundred cartons, the correspondence is a superb mirror of poets and their work for much of the twentieth century. One can read the era's history of poetry in a single body of correspondence.

Finally, there is fan mail. Often, this is simply letters the writer received but never answered. Such mail can give a clear indication of the writer's audience, or at least a segment of it, and reader's reactions to the writer's works. In some cases, the writer kept this mail. Sometimes, he responded to much of it. The materials can be found in files, as in the case of Frost, or pasted into albums, as in the case of Kenneth Roberts. If the material is in files, the careful use of sampling techniques can provide important data and, at the same time, cut down on a very bulky part of the collection. Many writers keep separate files of letters from cranks. Kenneth Roberts kept such a file, he carefully labeled "Nut Letters," for each of his major publications. Such separate files may be retained simply because the writer clearly wished to segregate and retain the contents.

Legal, business, and financial documents constitute an important section of any writer's papers. Contracts with editors of magazines and publishers of books provide important information to the researcher. These papers can act as a barometer of interest in the writer at any given time. If contracts or offers of contracts exist, this indicates that the writer was doing well. If the offers escalated, then the researcher can be certain that the writer was being courted because the public was buying his work.

Tax records are also a useful tool for studying the relative interest the public has in the work of a writer. It is possible to follow, for example, the rise in the fortunes of a writer simply by studying his tax returns. These records also show that many writers do not earn their livings from writing. Robert Frost did not earn much money from his writing, but he was able to make a comfortable living lecturing and reading his poems—what he called "barding about." All these records should be retained in the collection to enable the researcher to understand the financial pressures under which the writer worked.

Business records, such as bills and receipts, are bulky and contribute little to the research value of a collection. It is perhaps nice to know that Frost spent several dollars on stationery in Florida in January 1952, but this sort of information is of no real use to the researcher and only contributes to the bulk of the collection. When an author has been deified, archivists may be inclined to retain every scrap of material that relates to the writer simply so that the writer's every movement can be known. This, however, is not the best approach to appraising a collection.

The question of whether canceled checks should be retained can be argued from both points of view. Checks do provide some financial information and biographical details, such as what hotel the writer stayed at on a given night, but the data given are so negligible that checks should, in almost every case, be removed from a collection. The debate about checks remains open; there has been no concensus regarding their retention. If the decision is made to remove the checks, some care is required. Frost's canceled checks, for example, are worth fifty dollars on the autograph market.

The personal papers, that is, the nonliterary papers, of a writer are often merged with other parts of the collection. If separate, the papers may consist of correspondence, family legal documents, diaries, family photographs, and the like. These must be retained for the biographical data they contain. Copies of family papers or photographs that do not shed light on the writer or the writer's work can be removed with little difficulty and no harm to the integrity of the collection. The archivist must make retention decisions about other personal papers on a case-by-case basis. The decision to dispose of these materials must be based on their lack of substantive biographical information.

Poets seem to acquire copies of their work that have been used or manipulated by others. The five published musical versions of Frost's "Stopping by Woods on a Snowy Evening" or the three printed settings of "The Road Not Taken" are excellent examples of this. A number of settings are by noted composers; others are, at best, amateurish attempts for a single performance. Tapes and manuscripts of the latter have little research value and are best removed from the collection. Frost's papers contained a half-dozen tapes and scores of the sort that desperately demanded discarding. Tapes of performances and manuscripts of well-known composers should, of course, be retained.

Many writers are also educators in the formal sense. Papers that relate to their teaching function tend to be voluminous and of small consequence. Much of the material can be deleted or added to other parts of the collection. Term papers, grade records, and course outlines usually are of little consequence in the study of the writer and the writer's work. If the writer is influential, however, there may be some extremely important materials among these papers. An example of this occurs in the teaching papers of Richard Eberhart. At one of his first teaching positions, Eberhart taught English in a private school in Massachusetts. His prize pupil was Robert Lowell, later recognized as a great poet. The papers of Eberhart as a teacher of Lowell are of some importance because they include some of Lowell's early poetry, prose, and correspondence. It is necessary, clearly, to study this part of a collection with care and knowledge.

Publicity material that relates to the writer is found in abundance in many collections. Photographs, publicity clippings, and book reviews are important to the writer. Are they, however, important to the collection? Photographs, once the duplicates are removed, should be evaluated as a group. The appraiser should consider whether it is truly important to retain seventeen photographs of the writer in the same general pose at the same general age. One should suffice. A rigorous weeding of this part of the collection is definitely in order. Publicity clippings should also be weeded rigorously, particularly if the writer used a clipping service that clipped the same article from thirty-three different newspapers. Reviews present a problem. Many curators and archivists retain them in the collection, while an equal number opt for handing them to the rare-book librarian for addition in the collection of the writer's printed materials. Reviews can easily be retained in a collection if the papers are so organized that each work is treated separately. When there is a series of files on a particular book, from rough notes to page proofs, reviews fit nicely into the scheme.

Otherwise, it may be better to remove reviews from the papers. Consultation with the rare-book librarian may aid in making sound decisions in this area.

One particularly large group of material found in the papers of popular or successful writers is unsolicited manuscripts. Every writer develops a following that includes aspiring writers. These aspirants tend to send their work for discussion, criticism, and suggestions on how to get them published. Most writers quickly retire these manuscripts to the rubbish heap, but some let them accumulate and transfer them, unsorted and forgotten, to an institution. A rapid but careful sorting of these materials by someone who is capable of recognizing the names of a wide range of authors can easily sort the manuscripts that need to be saved from those that should be discarded. In most cases, the shredder is the most merciful place for unsolicited manuscripts. Many curators wonder whether the changing fortunes of some writers may require the retention of all unsolicited manuscripts. An author may be ignored or neglected for many years and then suddenly be discovered or rediscovered. This writer's early manuscripts may well have been sent to another writer for consideration and then been discarded by an appraiser as inappropriate to the collection of the other writer's papers. This, however, so rarely occurs that it is not worthy of excessive concern.

One of the first rules of thumb taught to processors is that every collection should have a miscellaneous category, or it has been overly processed and time and money have been wasted. In a writer's papers, the miscellaneous category can be anything from odd papers that defy description and placement to an ivory chess set. Much if not all of this material should be removed from the collection because it adds nothing to the researcher's knowledge of the writer.

Appraisal Approaches

Is there a common denominator for all literary collections? Clearly there is. Yet how a collection should be approached is determined by its type and the author himself. Manuscripts and correspondence will invariably be found, but research material or personal papers cannot always be located. Publicity and legal papers are usually present, but teaching papers are not always available. The thread that ties a collection together is the material upon which the writer depended—manuscripts and audience.

In considering the commonality of collections, one must also consider the treatment of collections. This is neither the time nor place to be even-handed or democratic. A collection such as the papers of Robert Frost should not be approached with the same frame of reference used to approach the collection of a writer who published poetry only in the local weekly paper. A different approach is clearly needed. An error in treating the papers of the local poet will not have the same effect as discarding the unknown, unrecognized draft of a major poet's attempt at a novel. Care and consideration must be the watchwords when processing the papers of a noted writer.

It must be noted, however, that the work of a major writer is much easier to appraise than the papers of an excruciatingly minor poet. For most known writers, there is a biography, or at least a biographical sketch, available, and, in some cases, there exists a bibliography that will enable the appraiser to determine published and unpublished materials as well as states of texts. Other tools may also be available, and using all such tools will enable the appraiser to make as sound a judgment as possible regarding the papers.

Some quarters voice the opinion that the papers of all writers must be considered equally important. The argument states that a minor writer might find late or posthumous fame and, therefore, all writers' papers must be treated with equal care. This viewpoint would appear to create a less than ideal situation for appraisers, whose judgments must be made on the basis of the quality of the writer as determined by literary critics and historians.

There are or seem to be two schools of appraisers. The first is the save-it-all school. Subscribers to this school believe that every scrap and shred of material must be retained just in case it may be of use to someone at some future date. How can one, for example, discard materials of a writer who was beatified during life and canonized after death? The pressure to save all the papers of such a person can be enormous. Frost is a prime example of a writer who was lionized and is still fondly remembered by several generations of Americans. Can anything of his be discarded?

The other school of appraisers is the bare-bones school. These appraisers remove anything that is not entirely germane to the collection. Photographs, any printed material (including galley and page proofs), clippings, and other detritus should be discarded to pare the collection down to a minimum. This type of appraisal is deemed successful only if the collection is boiled down to less than one-half its original size.

There is, of course, a middle ground. A large amount of material that comes in with an author's collection should not be taking up expensive time and valuable space. It must be removed if the collection is to be properly processed and made available to the public. Judicious appraisal of a literary collection will improve intellectual access to the material and make it more sensible to the researcher. This should be the goal of every appraisal.

One of the crucial problems facing any archivist or manuscript curator is determinating what is important in a collection and what is not. For example, the archivist processing Richard Eberhart's papers found a mass of manuscript material and printed papers relating to aerial gunnery. Under normal circumstances, the archivist would have removed this material from the collection on the basis that it was barely relevant. However, Eberhart wrote an important poem, "The Fury of Aerial Bombardment," which is elucidated and clarified by the papers from the gunnery school.[7] It is important, then, that the appraiser be familiar with the general history and criticism of the genre in which the papers fall, the history of the period, and, most important, the life and work of the author. Without such knowledge, important papers could be separated from the collection while, at the same time, useless papers might be retained. When looking at a contemporary body of literary papers, the appraiser should try to consider the concerns of the literary historians and critics of a century from now.

Disposition

The disposition of materials must be considered during the appraisal of a collection. The difficulty in doing this is being certain that the cash value of the materials does not influence the appraisal process. There can be a great temptation to gut a collection to pay for its processing and storage. At the same time, the archivist can be tempted to retain materials simply because they have monetary value; whether they contribute to the value of the entire collection may not be considered. Should all of Robert Frost's canceled checks be retained simply because they have value on the autograph market? Or should the market be flooded with these checks? The value of the materials should in no way be permitted to determine what is retained in a collection.

While disposition ought to be considered during the appraisal process the best method of disposition should not be determined until after appraisal is complete. Several fundamental questions regarding the material must be answered to determine the method of disposition. Are there written or oral agreements made with the donor or the estate of the creator of the papers? Will disposing of some materials affect other possible donations? Are there ethical questions to be considered? If there are no impediments to simply disposing of the unwanted material, then it can be done in the manner most suited to both the collection and the institution.

It would be delightful if what was removed from a collection could be sold and the profits used to cover the cost of appraisal, processing, and storage. This rarely happens. Instead, material is disposed of in one of several ways. The first method is simply shredding the material and disposing of the residue. This is an excellent method if the papers contain sensitive materials or materials that could be potentially embarrassing to others. A good candidate for shredding would be the grade records kept by a writer.

Shredding is also a useful disposition of materials that are of no value or interest to anyone. A second method of disposition is to transfer the materials to a different department within the institution. Books and printed records could go to the appropriate librarian, while institutional records could be integrated into the archives of the institution. Materials could also be given to another institution if they would be more appropriately housed there. The manuscript another poet sent for consideration might, for example, be more appropriately contained in the collection of that other poet.

The final possible method of disposition is, in fact, sale of the materials by private treaty, to a dealer, or through an auction house. Very often, literary papers are valuable enough that they can be sold to a dealer in autographs. The curator must be certain that the institution has the right to dispose of such materials by sale, that there are no ethical impediments, that the sale will not be an embarrassment to either the writer or the institution, and, finally, that the funds realized from the sale will be returned to the curator to fund the processing or further development of the collection.

Conclusion

The keys to a sound appraisal of literary manuscripts are knowledge of the writer, knowledge of the genre and period, and an understanding of the materials that make up the collection. An understanding of how and why certain materials can be utilized by students and scholars is also very useful. All this knowledge can then be drawn on during the critical process of appraisal. Without appraisal, the masses of paper found in many literary collections may deter researchers and will make intellectual access and bibliographic control impossible. Sound appraisal, however, will make literary collections both usable and useful.

Notes

1. Richard Eberhart, *Of Poetry and Poets* (Urbana: University of Illinois Press, 1979), p. xiii.

2. J. Albert Robbins, ed., *American Literary Manuscripts*, 2d ed. (Athens: University of Georgia Press, 1977). See entry under Robert Frost.

3. Because this writer and his institution must deal with the firms in question, their names will not be mentioned.

4. Stanford University Libraries. Collection Development Office. *Collection Development Policy Statement, 1980.* (Stanford, 1981).

5. Eberhart, pp. 302-303. This section of the book offers an interesting series of comments on the writing process in general.

6. This and all further examples cited are from collections in the Dartmouth College Library.

7. Eberhart, pp. 40-41.

6 Deaccessioning Collections: A New Perspective on a Continuing Controversy

Lawrence Dowler

The debate over deaccessioning is a principled dispute, one that might be more fruitful if only a less emotional and, to many, a less pejorative term could be coined. It would be sad, however, if either disdain for the term or fear of criticism should dissuade archivists from considering the implications of deaccessioning or prevent them from making the decisions they must make if they are to serve the purposes of research institutions and not curiosities. To be sure, one ought to be wary of the rapacious administrator, trustee, or politician—one thinks of the reputed threat of then Governor Reagan to sell the collections of the Bancroft Library in order to pay for the operating expenses of the University of California. Equally irresponsible, though, is the failure to perceive deaccessioning as a legitimate function of appraisal and an essential and integral part of collection development. If archivists do not arm themselves with adequate principles or have the courage to act, others, perhaps less principled or, at least, not so well-informed, will very likely make the decisions for them.

The purpose of this chapter is to examine three aspects of deaccessioning.[1] First, there is an attempt to broaden the definition of deaccessioning, to present it as a function of appraisal and not just as a source of revenue. Seen in this light, deaccessioning is a legitimate and shared responsibility of curators and administrators working together to develop those principles and guidelines that will in the end serve the goals of the institution. Second, there is an examination of the sale of materials—the heart of the controversy, if not the substance of the issue—that includes a discussion of the sale of literary property as well as physical property. Third, some of the underlying ideas that may influence and even govern our attitudes toward selling library materials, especially the motives of those who are constitutionally opposed to such sales, are suggested. By expanding the discussion of deaccessioning and giving it a slightly different shape, it may be possible to remove some of the sting and emotion from the topic and thereby pave the way for future discussions of several important and related issues, such as appraisal, collection development, and access, all of which are fundamental to the future of research collections.

Concerns About Deaccessioning

Few topics are more likely to arouse heated debate among curators and librarians than that of deaccessioning. There has been a curious reluctance to discuss this issue in public forums, however. Several articles in the *Wilson Library Bulletin* have provided a partial antidote to this reticence about publicizing a private passion.[2] Yet when the Society of American Archivists' program committee proposed a session on deaccessioning for its annual meeting, the committee was unable to locate enough willing speakers and had to cancel the session. On four separate occasions, speakers who had initially been enthusiastic about the topic, and who held strong convictions on the subject, either declined the invitation or withdrew from participation after having accepted because they feared that their opinions might cause them difficulties with their own administrations. No doubt the furor over the sale of the Brasher Doubloon by Yale University and the proposed sale of paintings by the Fogg Museum at Harvard University had something to do with this reluctance to make public statements.

Despite the apparent controversy surrounding it, there is nothing new about deaccessioning. All libraries, including rare-book libraries, hold book sales, and some maintain rooms where duplicate or unwanted materials are sold. Famous collections have, albeit not without controversy, been sold at auction. Johns Hopkins, Yale, and Cornell have disposed of numismatic collections and there have been highly publicized sales of rare books and manuscript collections by the Pierpont Morgan Library, the General Theological Seminary, the Franklin Institute in Philadelphia, the Boston Athenaeum, and the John Carter Brown Library at Brown University, to name a few of the most famous recent sales.

Faced with rising costs, shrinking budgets, and a wayward economy, many institutions appear to be looking to their collections as a way to pay off deficits, complete buildings, and finance operations. Too few, in the eyes of their critics, have thought of sales as a way of funding new acquisitions. The result has been alarm among curators, librarians, faculty, and donors, who fear that decisions to sell will be made by uninformed administrators, without regard to loss of research materials.

So great has been the concern about deaccessioning that, in June 1981, Brown University convened a conference on the subject.[3] The conference provided one of the first forums for serious discussion of deaccessioning in recent memory. A variety of views were aired. For example, curators and librarians expressed fear that rapacious administrators were poised to raid their collections.[4] On the other hand, some collectors complained that the best materials were being locked away in libraries, greatly diminishing opportunities for collectors. Other collectors wondered if they might not share with dealers and auction houses opportunities to acquire duplicate materials that are offered in library sales.[5] The contention of some curators that the proceeds of sales must be used only for new acquisitions was countered by a trustee who suggested that perhaps climate control and conservation represented a legitimate use of the funds.[6] Reading between the lines and listening carefully to discussions in the corridors, perceptive observers might have detected the fierce competition between dealers and auction houses over the disposition of library holdings; heard warnings of certain loss for the unwary librarian; and even picked up on the hint that those librarians who failed to honor the protocol of the book profession might expect to fare poorly in the marketplace.

Not all deaccessions are controversial. Some institutions have sold collections without incident or adverse public comment. While the Fogg Museum's proposal to sell art works was eventually dropped because of heavy protest, the Peabody Museum, just down the street from the Fogg, has financed more than half of a $4 million renovation from the sale of paintings, with little debate or acrimony.[7]

Although the sale of collections from archival repositories is uncommon, their deaccessioning of materials is not without precedent. The benign attitude toward deaccessioning may change as a result of the current suit against the Federal Bureau of Investigation (FBI) and the National Archives over the destruction of FBI records. But, prior to this case, there had been increasing discussion among archivists about disposing of collections as a necessary corollary to a sound appraisal plan.[8] Three deaccessioning decisions made by the Manuscripts and Archives Department of the Yale University Library may help to illustrate the nature of this relationship.

A few years ago, the Manuscript Division of the Library of Congress was astonished to receive a few boxes of the papers of Senator Robert Taft from the Yale University Library. Taft, after all, was a Yale man, and at the time, Horace Taft was dean of Yale College. However, the Taft Family papers were all at the Library of Congress and the decision to deaccession was made on the grounds that researchers should not be inconvenienced by Yale's retaining a few boxes of papers for reasons of institutional pride. One hastens to add that finding examples in which this spirit of charity and concern for the convenience of researchers has not prevailed is far from difficult. Few institutions easily part with, what Tom Wolfe has called the right stuff.

Yale gave a valuable collection of files documenting the activities of the Hoe Company, one of the most important companies in the history of U.S. printing, to Columbia University. Columbia held the majority of that company's records and has, as one of its major collection areas, the history of printing. Yale's own collections on this subject are not insignificant. Both the Beinecke Library and the Arts of the Book Collection in Sterling Library contain outstanding representations of the history of printing, as well as fine presses and the files of several important printers and publishers. But Yale had not concentrated on commercial printing, although one might argue that it should. Consequently, it was decided that scholarship would be better served if the files were united, even though the consolidation would be at another institution.

Several years ago, the University of Connecticut launched an archival program with the announced intention of collecting Connecticut history, especially on the subjects of business and labor history. Yale greeted the arrival of what might have been viewed as a competitor with open arms and two truckloads of Connecticut business records. This response was not without self-interest, because Yale, like most repositories, was short of space and, in truth, was no longer interested in collecting business records. In fact, Yale had previously sent several large collections of Connecticut business records to the Baker Library at Harvard. Yale welcomed the University of Connecticut Archives, too, because, in a state with a long and proud manufacturing tradition, there were few large repositories able to share in the collecting of such records.

Each of the preceding examples of deaccessioning is susceptible to arguments against disposal. In the case of the Taft papers, institutional pride would have been a powerful reason for retention; for the Hoe Company records, it would have been easy to argue for retention on the grounds of related collection strength. In the case of the Connecticut business collections, one might have argued for retention because the records document the history of Connecticut, a subject in which Yale has great collection strength. An even more compelling reason for retaining these papers would have been the fact that, at the time of the transfer, two Yale students were using materials in these collections in their dissertations, and a prominent member of the university administration, an economic historian, also had scholarly interest in them.

It is worth noting that all of the examples of deaccessioning cited, while occasionally prompting astonishment on the part of the recipients, never aroused any interest, let alone adverse comment, on the part of anyone in the university. This climate of benign acceptance changed rather dramatically in 1981, when Yale sold the Brasher Doubloon for a princely sum, planning to use the proceeds of the sale to pay for the bricks and mortar of a new storage library. The sale prompted a hue and cry from some faculty and alumni. A memorandum addressed to the president by three faculty members denounced the sale as a barbarous act. Several alumni, of the sort university presidents generally pay some attention to, threatened to never again donate anything to the institution that would do such a terrible thing. Parenthetically, some equally prominent alumni, no doubt hard-headed businessmen, applauded the sale as a long-overdue step toward self-help. Still, after this sale, there was a new awareness of the problems of selling collections and the responsibility entailed in accepting them.

The immediate result of the Brasher Doubloon sale, apart from providing the necessary funds to complete the building of a desperately needed library, was a prohibition against the sale of any university property until a committee of the corporation could produce a decision-making policy for all future deaccessions. Following a year of deliberation, a policy was issued requiring that all future sales and, more important for the future of collection development, all large acquisitions be approved by the provost. It is ironic that purchased acquisitions, large or small, were exempted from this required approval. In spite of this restriction, the library later sold both art works and duplicate books, although curators and librarians would, no doubt, think twice about selling library property in the future and, on the other hand, perhaps be more cautious about accepting it. One wonders what impact this policy will have on future collection development and, more important, on the role of curators and librarians in the implementation of such development.

If deaccessioning has such a long history, why the sudden furor? There are probably several reasons, all of them emotionally charged and difficult to document. These are hard times for libraries and nonprofit institutions. There is the legitimate fear that, in response to financial pressure, hard-pressed administrators and trustees, who are often perceived as ignorant of and occasionally indifferent to cultural and humanistic values, will sell their institution's treasures without a thought to future scholarship. Moreover, there is a perceptible growth in the mistrust of administrative superiors—curators and others responsible for building collections sense more and more that they are being opposed by a class of managers who are more at home with computers and financial statements than they are with the library's collections or its mission. Certainly, this is a perception shared by many faculty members, who see themselves as apart from, if not opposed to, the administrators of the institution that they are both paid to serve. These perceptions and feelings seem to fuel the misapprehension with which so many regard the matter of deaccessioning.

Some critics of deaccessioning may not, however, be as hostile to its objectives as the heat of the debate and the language of their opposition sometimes suggest. When pushed, some who oppose selling collections will acquiesce if they know that the proceeds from the sale are to be used for additional acquisitions. It is when decisions are made to sell materials in order to provide operating funds, pay salaries, or, worse, pay heating bills or provide bricks and mortar for a new building that principles are involved and a call to arms is issued.

The Role of the Curator

Lurking beneath the surface of the dispute over deaccessioning, in particular the quarrel over the proper use of funds obtained from the sale of collections, lies a hidden assumption. Namely, that curatorial responsibility ends with the acquisition of collections. In short, curators have been far too willing to assume that the administration, the library, the university, or anyone but themselves is responsible for providing support for the materials that they have acquired.

This point deserves comment, both because it has important implications for special collections and because it lies at the heart of the argument about deaccessioning. The notion that curatorial responsibility is principally concerned with acquisitions and not operations is characteristic of what might be called the connoisseur approach to special collections. A connoisseur is the curator with a keen appreciation for his collection, who is generally knowledgeable about its contents, and is, therefore, a good guide for researchers. For the most part, the connoisseur is not terribly concerned with administrative procedures. The relationship of the special collection to the library or institution as a whole is generally far from the connoisseur's waking thoughts.

A more realistic curator views special collections, not as an independent fiefdom, but as an integral part of the research library. This type of curator sees himself as a partner in the enterprise. Such a curator might be called a managerial librarian or archivist; that is, one who organizes and manages a collection and assumes some responsibility and, yes, risk for its support and integration into the larger institution of which it is a part. For the manager, knowledge of the collection is still essential, but so too is seeking the support of students, faculty, friends, and perhaps even financial sources. Access is just as important as collection development to the managerial curator. The relationship of the collection to curriculum and the needs of the university share a place with the preservation of the artifacts of culture and civilization.

The contrast between the connoisseurial and managerial approaches to special collections is perhaps best illustrated by the recent concern voiced by rare-book librarians about what they perceive to be their diminished status within universities. The evidence most often cited to support this contention is the alleged failure of universities to support special collections, particularly rare books, at the level to which many repositories had grown accustomed during the golden age of the 1950s. All library activities and budgets have come under the scrutiny of university administrators in recent financially difficult years, but there is more here than a complaint about finances. At issue is the sense that university administrators, and even the librarians, are no longer as sympathetic to the purposes of special collections as they once had been. Under the old order, there was a presumption of sympathy and support for the aims of special collections. Not only did the administration assume that a special collection was valuable—rarely was anyone asked to justify its existence or explain its purpose in relation to that of the university or the library—but very often it was perceived as the flagship of the library and a beacon for attracting support. The special-collections connoisseur still clings to this perception—it was, after all, a successful model in the past—and seems unable to grasp that the political and economic realities of the present demand some accommodations. If, however, archivists and curators are not to be captive of attitudes of the recent past, they also must not be captive of the administrative structures of the past. They need a new model, the special-collections manager who not only will give reasons for his collection and define its relationship to the institution of which it is part, but who is willing to build a new constituency of users and donors to help sustain the collection in the future.

Deaccessioning as a Function of Appraisal

It seems pointless to argue categorically against the disposal of collections and even less useful to contend that the decision to sell materials is the exclusive prerogative of the curator, librarian, or administrator. All curators, archivists, and librarians recoil from the most blatant examples of raids upon the treasures of a library. But, in their desire to protect the integrity of collections, they ought not lose sight of the need to "continually re-examine . . . appraisal policies in light of changing and expanding research requirements."[9] While acknowledging the obligation to donors and the legal limitations of disposal, they must also recognize that libraries, no less than collectors, may buy, trade, sell, and dispose of materials in an effort to upgrade and improve or simply change the focus of their collections. In any case, deaccessioning is an appropriate part of appraisal, and the sale of collections—of duplicate or out-of-scope materials—is a legitimate method for achieving this end. The enormous growth of information gives impetus to the demand for informed judgments about what to save and what to discard. As Herb Finch has observed, "How much space and money can we expect society to provide for the care of its records? . . . And at what point do we start reducing the pile so that the pursuit of knowledge is not hampered?"[10]

The appropriate use of proceeds from the sale of materials is, as this chapter has indicated, a volatile issue. Few serious people are suggesting that libraries and archives hold yard sales in order to balance the budget. However, the financing of operating expenses, that is, paying staff to maintain, service, preserve, and make collections accessible, is a legitimate use of funds obtained from the sale of unwanted materials. Recognizing this need, some institutions now encourage donors of acquisition endowments to set aside 25 percent of the endowment for the maintenance of the collection, and most institutions now refuse to accept a gift of buildings and property without an adequate endowment to support its operation. The Peabody Museum's decision to use the proceeds from the sale of paintings to renovate its space will permit it to meet one of its primary purposes, that of saving material from those cultures no longer extant. The Peabody's paintings did not serve this purpose, and the museum's director, C.C. Lamgerg-Karlosvky, is " . . . convinced that the benefit derived far exceeds the maintenance of those collections that did not provide us any essential role in research or teaching in the Museum of Department of Anthropology."[11] No doubt there are those who would still oppose the sale, but who can fault the justification for this decision to deaccession? The point is that each decision to deaccession must be considered, case by case, in accordance with the moral and legal obligations of the institution, as well as its current purposes.

There are those who contend that an institution acquires an eternal obligation to retain the collections it accepts and that the sale of materials may have a detrimental effect on future donations.[12] There is no denying that the the publicity surrounding the sale or disposal of collections may prompt some donors to withhold future gifts or withdraw current deposits. The most obvious response to this problem is for an institution to honestly acknowledge the vicissitudes of life and the possibility of an altered mission or changed financial climate. Statements that acknowledge these possibilities and allow for the future disposition of collections, if this becomes necessary or is deemed desirable, should be part of the institution's acquisition policy and may also be incorporated into the deed of gift. If the possibility of deaccessioning is a matter of concern to the donor, then the deed of gift should frankly acknowledge this concern and state the terms governing disposal. For example, it might stipulate that the collection must be returned to the donor's heirs, placed in another repository, or offered for sale only to certain individuals or institutions. In any case, it is interesting to note that the only attempt to survey donors on this issue, of which this writer is aware, produced a much more favorable response than might have been expected, given the emotional responses one has become accustomed to hearing.[13]

To those who contend that deaccessioning removes materials forever from the world of scholarship, it should be pointed out that many of today's great research collections in libraries are the gifts of devoted private collectors who have donated their collections to institutions, often with an endowment to maintain them. It was not, after all, an institution that recently rescued a copy of the Declaration of Independence from removal to England, but a private collector who purchased the document and presented it to a library. Indeed, the role of collectors in building the great research collections in this country is not as well-known or understood as it ought to be.

The point here is not to defend the marketplace or even collectors. Rather, the aim is to provide a more balanced presentation of that which critics often characterize as a pernicious mercantile spirit. Many curators and librarians have reservations about the relationship of research materials to commerce, and most are grateful that a large body of research materials has not yet fallen prey to the marketplace. There is, however, no convincing argument that research and scholarship will come to an end if the materials are sold.

To those who would argue that there is no such thing as a duplicate book,[14] and therefore none should be sold, it can only be asserted that, while there are numerous cases to support this contention, it is an overstated argument that reflects only one among several kinds of bibliographic approaches to the study of books. Further, if pursued to its logical conclusion, this argument quickly becomes absurd.[15] Of course, the decision to deaccession duplicate books must be made with care and a full knowledge that mistakes in judgment can and most certainly will be made. Would any archivist or librarian admit to anything less in considering decisions to acquire these materials in the first place? One has only to attend a rare-book fair and observe dealers buying from one another to understand that such transactions occur because the buyer knows or thinks he knows something the seller does not, if only that there is a customer waiting for precisely this item. Indeed, tales of the exchanges comprise the lore of the book trade and occassionally incite the novice to take up the chase.

Rapid changes in technology may further challenge current assumptions about deaccessioning materials. One wonders, for example, what the impact of video-disc technology will have on deaccessioning. If valuable information can be retained in a permanent form, will archivists still feel obliged to retain original materials that have little value as objects? Given the possibility of alternative forms of storing information and the enormous cost of climate controls and space, they may decide, as have some libraries, to let the originals decay. This, too, is a decision to deaccession. Perhaps the current effort of the Public Archives of Canada to record all its records on video discs will also prompt them to provide guidelines and a model for deciding what to preserve and what to discard.

The decision to deaccession is a difficult one, but it is precisely the informed appraisal decision that finally distinguishes the professional from the technician. One longs for eternal verities, but the nature of education is to seek them or, rather, to learn how to seek them, and librarians and archivists, no less than scholars, must attempt to serve that enterprise through collection-development policies that include the periodic reappraisal of current practices and past decisions. One must simply acknowledge that the criteria for collecting research materials does change, and so do the needs of the institution. Collections must be administered and preserved, but not as if they were sacraments. Responsible curators, archivists, and librarians must constantly interpret and evaluate their collections as forces in a collection plan, and not as a part of immutable law sanctioned by Holy Writ.

The Sale of Copyright

Until now, the chapter has focused on the disposition of physical property. Another issue, equally controversial, and one that many archivists and librarians will have to consider sooner than they think, is the sale of literary rights or, more precisely, the copyright in research collections.

There is a clear distinction between ownership of physical property and ownership of the words or images in a collection. Many librarians and archivists have been diligent in recent years in trying to acquire the copyright in materials, principally as a way of simplifying for researchers the task of obtaining permission to publish. As a result of this hard work, they are about to be rewarded with a host of complex legal and ethical problems that are not totally unrelated to the question of selling collections. True, they will not have to decide whether the sale of a unique item may violate their obligation to preserve the intellectual and cultural heritage of the nation, but they may have to decide on the sale of the use of a property that is unique and bears an important and subtle relationship to the question of access.

Everyone has heard that the video and computer revolution has begun. Prophetic articles appearing in popular magazines state that the United States, indeed, the world, will very shortly be wired for video. If the buzz word of the early sixties was "plastics" and the seventies, "software," the byword of the eighties probably will be "cable."

A recent advertisement for a workshop on cable television reported that, by the spring of 1983, 80 to 85 percent of the greater Boston area would be licensed for cable television, representing more than 160 communities and a population of over 3 million people.[16] Large sums of money are being spent to acquire new properties. Home Box Office (HBO) spent well over $3 million in the production of Lerner and Lowe's *Camelot*. The Entertainment Channel (TEC) is reported to have spent $1.8 million producing *Pippin* and $1.5 million producing *Sweeney Todd*. Cable sales may be a significant new source of income for playwrights. Arthur Miller, for example, reportedly negotiated the sale of his *A View from the Bridge* for $800,000.[17]

Although it is too early to predict with certainty the future relationship of cable and theater, at the moment it appears likely that cable will play an important, perhaps even dominant, role in theater. With production costs soaring, cable could become the primary patron of the theater. Whether cable becomes an "angel" for the theater, that is, assumes the risks for untried theatrical productions, remains to be seen. What appears more certain is that cable's appetite for fresh programing will send it scurrying after new sources.[18]

Why is this important for archives and libraries? For one thing, the cable industry is principally an entertainment industry—at least, this is the current major source of its income. And, as an entertainment industry, it has an insatiable appetite for properties—for plays, dramatizations, documentaries, and the like. Many of these properties are owned—more than one may realize—by libraries and archival repositories. The question is whether curators and librarians will be prepared to either service requests for, say, the dramatization of an historical event for which their institution holds the primary documentation or, more to the point, profit from its use?

Like the author whose property may have been acquired, a library is in a position either to profit from the sale of copyright and publication rights or be victimized by the unintentional loss of those rights. For example, the first and second *Superman* movies reportedly made $184 million for its producers and not one cent for the original creator, at least not until a successful lawsuit produced some belated compensation for the author. Publishing contracts do not automatically cover other forms of production, such as motion-picture, video, or cable films, any more than acquiring physical property automatically includes the acquisition of literary rights. What is more, in largely derivative media, such as television, the notion of intellectual property becomes even more obscure and even less defensible than claims based on the printed page. For example, in the American Broadcasting Company's program, "Greatest American Hero," the hero wears a cape, has x-ray vision, and flies through the air in a manner so familiar that the current owner of Superman filed suit on the grounds that its intellectual property had been stolen.[19]

Consider another case. If a made-for-television movie is produced from the recent biography of Walter Lippmann instead of from the papers that are owned by Yale University, the library will presumably derive little or no financial benefit from the movie, even though the book was based almost entirely on the collection for which Yale owns the copyright. Given the kind of scholarly use generally made of its collections, the library can hardly be faulted for failing to anticipate or profit from the enormous popular success of the book. Even if it had, however, it is unlikely that anyone could have predicted then that parts of the book might be adapted for a television production. This is simply not a question people working in an academic environment were then, or even now, likely to ask.

Of course, not everyone owns the copyright to an important and profitable author's work, but, as suggested earlier, an institution may possess more valuable property than it realizes. A few years ago, for example, a major network was reported to have paid an attorney for the plaintiffs in the Kent State case $400,000 just for permission to use his research notes. If an institution had owned these notes, would its administrators have been prepared to negotiate such a lucrative agreement on its behalf? Or might the response have been that the curator's role was simply to make these materials available for research, regardless of the purpose for which they would be used? The way this question is answered has profound policy implications for research collections and for librarians, archivists, or curators.

What must also be realized when thinking about these issues is that a particular production on television will not only have a one-time showing in its country of origin but may also have repeated showings throughout the world. Who will represent the library or repository in this legal thicket? Not only do institutions need legal representation in preparing contracts, specifically contracts covering each type of use of a property (for example, publication, motion picture film, video and cable rights), but their administrators must also ask who will monitor such productions in order to collect royalties and ensure that contracts are not violated? Finally, the administrators must recognize that, while they may be fortunate enough to find a lawyer capable of preparing a proper contract, what they will want and need specifically is an agent to promote the properties in which they have an active interest. At the moment, such qualified agents can literally be counted on the fingers of one hand. In addition, those who are available stand to make enormous profits in the commercial sector and are, therefore, unlikely to work for a library or university, at least, not under the customary salary arrangements offered by most institutions.

What is meant by promotion? Quite literally, it is the marketing and selling of literary properties for publication, performance (in the case of plays), or dramatization for television and cable. A number of institutions do own important literary properties, and percentage-of-royalty arrangements are likely to become more common in the future as repositories seek ways to support and maintain the collections entrusted to their care. Yale, for example, owns the copyright for many of Eugene O'Neill's plays and enjoys income from the publication and production of these works. With proper promotion, it is likely that such income could be increased substantially. On the other hand, if these properties are not monitored and protected, potential income will be lost. The idea that an institution should seek to protect and actively promote its interest is contrary to the academic ethos and may be a major stumbling block to the most pertinent question, which is, how does a library or university protect its interests in these matters?

One possibility would be for universities to establish corporations to manage their literary properties or to establish the kinds of linkages with commercial firms that several institutions have created in order to market their scientific discoveries. Whether the potential profits from library materials warrant this kind of enterprise remains to be seen. What is clear is that most institutions are limited in their ability to protect their intellectual rights and are, therefore, vulnerable to commercial exploitation in a rapidly changing entertainment and communications industry.

The idea of promoting literary properties is not something any archivist or librarian ever contemplated when joining the field; indeed, the very thought of selling literary property may be as repugnant to some as the thought of selling collections. Curators imagine themselves to be builders of collections, protectors of a cultural heritage, and an integral part of the research process. Consider this question, however: if a library owns the copyright of, say, an author's plays, is it thereby obliged to try to have them performed? A curator's primary role may be to make materials available for research, but a playwright writes plays in order to have them performed. As the owner of a play, is an institution also responsibile for promoting it, that is, selling it and making sure that it is performed? Certainly, some librarians and archivists think that one of their professional responsibilities is to publish research collections, whether in a printed form or microform, presumably in order to make the materials more easily accessible to students and scholars. Does this responsibility change or become tainted if the publication or performance happens to be profitable?

The question that must be asked—and it is an ethical as well as a legal question—is whether an academic institution ought to profit from the commercial use of its resources. The answer to this question is neither obvious nor easy; indeed, it raises further, fundamental questions about the very nature and purpose of an institution.

The most obvious danger in embracing the idea of promotion is that institutions may choose collections with an eye toward potential profits rather than their value for research. In one sense, accepting collections for their potential financial benefit is an old custom among librarians. Few institutions find it possible to refuse a collection proffered by an important benefactor or wealthy alumnus. Still, there is a perceptible difference between a display of sensitivity toward a valued friend of an institution and the hot pursuit of a collection that has little to recommend it except its promise to turn a profit.

This potential danger to the library and the university or college of which it is a part bears a strong resemblance to the danger posed by the availability of money to the faculty of sciences in the university. The wide availability of money, most recently for genetic research, has been called by Derek Bok, president of Harvard University, the "marijuana of the eighties." The danger, he said, is that professors will choose research topics for financial rather than scientific value and that "Universities may make compromising decisions [about scientific programs] based more on an effort to make money than on scientific merit."[20] While it is hard to imagine anyone in the humanities, least of all in the library, confronted by such Faustian temptations, the lure of money is nevertheless real, and its potential for mischief should not be underestimated.

There is always the danger, too, that, once would-be donors discover the potential for profit in their papers, they may be tempted either to retain their collections for themselves or place legal restrictions on publication and perhaps access that could create an onerous burden on the recipient institution. The changes in the tax laws, which deny a tax benefit to the creator of a collection for the donation of his collection to a nonprofit institution, has severely limited donations. What is more, this tax-law revision appears to have created a sellers' market for literary manuscripts and even some historical collections. It is quite possible that the growing market for new properties to feed cable programing will have the same effect. Repositories may, however, be able to counter this trend by offering creative new contracts or legal instruments that serve to preserve valuable collections for research purposes while assuring both the donors and the institutions a fair percentage of royalties from the commercial use of the collections. The point is, archives and libraries must be prepared to take advantage of financial opportunities when they occur, while avoiding being victimized by commercial exploitation of their resources. Many institutions have already taken a step in this direction by raising facsimile reproduction fees for the use of photographs in order to discourage the commercial exploitation of their collections by publishers who wish to avoid the higher charges of commercial photographic archives. What repositories have not done, and perhaps cannot do, is to take the next step and openly compete with commercial archives in order to earn a profit from their collections.

The potential exploitation of research collections by commercial firms raises several important questions about the traditional policies of access, the ways in which publications are monitored and, indeed, the very purpose of such collections. It may be that a distinction must be made between the kinds of use made of collections. This, in turn, will require that the terms of access to collections be clarified. Should a staff person from a cable network or television station doing research for a dramatization be allowed the same access as that given to the student working on a dissertation? Anyone who has ever witnessed the disruption or endured the demands for service by, say, a television producer, will readily understand this distinction. Forgetting for a moment the question of whether a library or archives should attempt to profit from the sale of its collections, one must simply ask if the different purposes for which collections are used does not, in the end, demand policies that acknowledge these differences. With the proper legal instruments, institutions may be able to protect their property rights and secure a proper return on various forms of publication and production. But should they not also make a distinction between scholarly research and the commercial use of collections, and perhaps charge for the latter use? The irony is that many librarians and archivists have worked hard to eliminate distinctions among researchers, mostly in order to avoid having to administer the kinds of exclusive access policies that were once common among libraries. If, however, the difference in the kinds of use made of collections is acknowledged and institutions declare their wish either to profit from commercial publication based on collections or at least avoid being victimized by such publications, a notion that many have worked hard to eliminate from deeds of gift—that is, the phrase "qualified researcher"—may be reintroduced. The use of the invidious adjective "qualified" was, in the past, a code word used to enforce the exclusion of anyone either the donor or the institution deemed unworthy. A better strategy is to open the gate, but charge those who are able to pay. In other words, institutions should charge for both the use of collections and for publications that are intended for commercial or profitable purposes. At the same time, repositories will need to obtain legal instruments that provide for some compensation for the commercial adaptation or transfer of a research product from one medium to another, for example, the television docudrama derived from a noncommercial publication.

Conclusion

It is impossible to predict the long-range implication of the economic, social, and technical changes that are now occurring. In these times of financial difficulty, it is imperative that libraries and archival institutions be at least as creative in finding ways to finance their operations as they have been in acquiring their collections. Curators and administrators need to be alert to new opportunities, while remaining ever mindful of their dangers. Deaccessioning, as it has been broadly described in this chapter, offers one such opportunity, although it is not without risks. The practice of any profession, if done by sensitive people, creates financial risks and moral dilemmas. The categorial opposition to deaccessioning or to the sale of intellectual property reflects a strong desire to eliminate those risks and moral dilemmas by self-imposed rules that narrow or suppress choices. Archivists ought to demand more of their profession and expect more from themselves. For, in the end, they will be judged by the way in which they respond to these changes and problems. The risks are great, but so too are the opportunities.

Notes

1. This chapter is based on a talk given at the annual meeting of the New England Archivists in Mystic, Connecticut, on May 15, 1982.

2. Peter Modell, "Books at Auction: The Art of Deaccessioning," *Wilson Library Bulletin* 56 (September 1981): 33-38; Samuel Streit, "Research Library Deaccessioning: Practical Considerations," *Wilson Library Bulletin* 56 (May 1982): 658-662; Daniel Traister, "Goodbye to All That: A Case Study in Deaccessioning," *Wilson Library Bulletin* 56 (May 1982): 663-668; Desmond Neill, "Defending Duplicates: The Value of Variant Copies," *Wilson Library Bulletin* 56 (May 1982): 669-672.

3. *Deaccession in Research Libraries, Papers Read at a Symposium Held at Brown University, June 11, 12, 1981* (Providence: 1981).

4. David H. Stam, " 'Prove All Things: Hold Fast That Which is Good,' Deaccessioning and Research Libraries," Ibid., pp. 9-13; Marcus McCorison, "Effects of Deaccession on Rare Book and Special Collections Libraries," Ibid., pp. 29-33.

5. Charles Tanenbaum, "Deaccessioning and the Collector: I," Ibid., pp. 47-50.

6. Augustus P. Loring, "Deaccession and the Board of Trustees," Ibid., pp. 17-18.

7. *Harvard Crimson*, 19 February 1983.

8. See, for example, Meyer H. Fishbein, "A Viewpoint on Appraisal of National Records," *American Archivist* 33 (April 1970): 175-187, and Leonard Rapport, "No Grandfather Clause: Reappraising Accessioned Records," *American Archivist* 44 (Spring 1981): 143-150.

9. Fishbein, "A Viewpoint," p. 175.

10. "Deaccessioning," *Documentation Newsletter VI*, no. 2 (Fall 1980): 4.

11. *Harvard Crimson*, 19 February 1983.

12. For various viewpoints, see Stam, " 'Prove All Things,' " pp. 4-12.

13. Robert Nikirk, "Deaccession and Donor Relations," *Deaccession in Research Libraries*, p. 34-37.

14. Neill, "Defending Duplicates;" Falconer Madan, "Duplicity of Duplication," *Transactions of the Bibliographical Society* 12 (1914): 15-24.

15. See for example Fredson Bowers's *Bibliography & Modern Librarianship* (Berkeley: School of Librarianship, University of California, 1966), pp. 21-22.

16. *Mecca Workshops*, 12 May 1982.

17. *New York Times*, 27 June 1982.

18. Ibid.

19. *New York Times*, 27 March 1983.

20. *The Harvard Independent*, 2 December 1982.

7

Archival Choices: Managing the Historical Record in an Age of Abundance

F. Gerald Ham

In November 1974, the distinguished historian John Hope Franklin stood before the bench in a federal courtroom in Chicago and stated his opinion regarding the merits of preserving the records of the past. One must save everything, he said, because "there's no way to know what's going to be valuble ten, fifteen or a hundred years from now."

The "everything" he referred to were the 1,507 boxes of assorted material that made up the gubernatorial papers of the Honorable Otto Kerner, Jr., former governor of Illinois, who was just then enjoying the shortest of leaves from a federal correctional facility in Lexington, Kentucky. Kerner's appraiser, Ralph Newman—of Nixon papers fame—had appraised the governor's papers in excess of $73,000. The Internal Revenue Service (IRS) contended that the papers would fetch a bit less than that in the "fair market." The IRS won its point.[1]

How simple it would be for archivists to follow Professor Franklin's dictum. If it cost nothing to accession and preserve records, they could save everything—no matter how trivial—and then, of course, archivists would have anticipated every conceivable research use. Society, however, would regard such broadness of spirit as profligacy, if not outright idiocy. Instead, archivists—like most residents of the real world—must pick and choose.

The Kerner papers underscore the problems—economic and otherwise—of managing the historical record with limited resources in an age when papers are produced in abundance. Some of these problems are well-known to archivists. Bulk is one; Governor Kerner amassed over 750 cubic feet of records during his eight years in office. Papers of nineteenth century governors held by the Illinois State Historical Library averaged ten cubic feet.[2]

Another problem is the redundancy of information in modern collections. Much of the data in such collections resemble more the noise and distortions of a badly tuned television set than useful information. One-hundred-and-five boxes of Kerner's papers, or approximately 52,000 items, were ceremonial invitations—many to snip ribbons at shopping centers.

Ironically, in spite of the bulk and redundancy of modern records, there is also a problem of missing data. What is missing from the Kerner papers, for example, is the governor himself. His papers, which are actually the records of the executive office, reveal almost nothing about the man, his thought processes, or his style of life, whether political or administrative.[3] These records are a prime example of how modern telecommunications have brought about the death of what can be called intimate recorded communication and reflection—the letter and the diary.

The impermanence of the modern record is still another problem in collection management. Many of Governor Kerner's papers were electrostatic copies, which have now faded beyond legibility. Modern technology has compounded this problem by producing records that are amendable, on mediums that are fragile and reusable. It is difficult to accession such records before the information they contain disappears.

The preservation of modern collections may be prohibitively expensive. Fourteen years after the records were acquired the Kerner files are still in a preliminary state of arrangement and description, and they are likely to remain that way. Recent cost analysis suggests that traditional processing of a collection of this size and complexity might easily cost more than $62,000.[4]

The most difficult and least-recognized problem that collection management must deal with is the structural bias in the national archival record. Accessions programs have loaded archival shelves with too much documentation on certain aspects of U.S. life and culture, and almost nothing on others. The Kerner files and associated collections of gubernatorial and congressional records in the same institution are a case in point; they comprise over 50 percent, or 4,500 of the 8,900 linear feet, of repository holdings.[5] As a result of the emphasis on these aspects, many other aspects of state history must necessarily go undocumented. As Jutta Scott-Reed has noted, this age of overabundant records and information, combined with an increasing scarcity of resources, is forcing archivists to replace their essentially unplanned approach to archival preservation with a "systematic, planned, documented process of building, maintaining, and preserving collections."[6]

This concept of collection management offers archivists a new way of thinking about their work. The concept suggests that the basic archival functions (appraisal, accessioning, arrangement, and conservation) are not discrete, isolated activities, but rather part of a process or continuum. A key feature of collection management is the conceptual integration of acquisition and processing functions into a single system.

Collection management must deal with records before they come into archival custody. Only by controlling what comes through their doors can archivists solve the major problems in modern records administration. They can do this by applying familiar ideas and practices more rigorously, by devising new and more sophisticated methods of selection and control, and by using their resources in a more planned and efficient way.

There are many important elements in archival collection management. Six will be discussed in this chapter: interinstitutional cooperation in collecting; disciplined and documented application of appraisal procedures; deaccessioning; prearchival control of records; record-volume reduction; and analysis and planning.

Interinstitutional Cooperation and Collection Building

The problem of structural bias in current archival holdings can be addressed through interinstitutional cooperation in collection building. It also enables archivists to make better use of limited resources to compile a more representative record of the past. To build such a record, archivists must alter their perspective on collection development. They need to look beyond an essentially introspective and isolated approach to archival accessioning and consider how individual institutional efforts might contribute to a broader regional and national historical collecting process.

To go beyond attitudinal changes to the coordination of collecting activities requires archivists to build interinstitutional linkages. How do they do this? They face a severe structural problem, because institutional archives exist to serve the administrative and other needs of the parent body, not an amorphous group called researchers. Furthermore, archivists' experience with interinstitutional cooperation is limited, and they have few guiding models or plans available. They lack such basic building blocks as well-articulated institutional accession statements. Most of all, they have insufficient data about current holdings nationwide to permit the kind of analysis that Jutta Reed-Scott contends is an essential precondition or prerequisite for program planning and development.

What they do have, however, are some new archival structures that should help archivists solve some of their problems. These structures are the statewide archival networks, such as the Minnesota Regional Research Centers, the Joint University-State Historical Society system in Missouri, and the Wisconsin Area Research Centers. Such regionally based centers, located on university campuses, serve as the archives, both public and private, for the surrounding multicounty area; they also serve faculty and students as well as a nonacademic constituency interested in family and community history. Usually, there is a core area of collecting that is common to all regional centers—politics, community development, biography, and so forth. These regional core collections, when combined, collectively create a statewide body of complementary holdings.[7]

Rather than build collections indiscriminately or redundantly, a collecting strategy can enable institutions to move beyond the complementary core collection to individual center specialization. Since, for the most part, each center serves a geographic region with different characteristics, each should have the opportunity to document these differences. Building subject collections on a geographic basis is not entirely a logical enterprise, yet it is here that the cooperative network structure can provide some rationality. In Minnesota, for example, the network members agreed that one center would document the activities of Depression-era farmer-protest groups, while another center would document ethnic customs among Scandinavians.[8] With limited resources for preserving the record, such rationalizations are not just common sense; they are imperative. Because collections are accessioned systematically, there is no wasteful competition. The interests of the researcher are better served, because such planned accessions allow archivists to do a better job at filling existing gaps in the historical record. In addition to providing more representative coverage, collecting models can also assist in the building of important bodies of comparative documentation. Historical records that appear to document fragmented or isolated phenomena often become more important when they can be plugged into parallel collections elsewhere.

The number of such statewide networks should be increased. In addition, new kinds of cooperation should be created. Cooperation should be based on institutional type, such as university, church, or state archives, and on subject, for example, labor, science, and technology.

Coordinated interinstitutional collecting requires careful planning and program phasing. A first phase should involve the collecting of information about holdings, accessions focus or policy, and acquisition procedures of all cooperating institutions. The implementation of cooperative collecting strategies and programs would be a second phase. A necessary third phase would include steps to ensure program continuation. This would require archivists to establish mechanisms for continuous information sharing, for monitoring, for conflict resolution, and for the modification and updating of policies and plans.

Disciplined Appraisal

Archivists must also refine their criteria and techniques for records selection at the institutional level. This second element of archival collection management calls for a more disciplined approach to appraisal. Here one might consider the radical position of the New York State Archives: when in doubt, leave it out. "If there is any archival 'principle' that delineates our appraisal activity," so reads their policy statement, "it is that any records are to be rejected unless there are definite and compelling justifications for their preservation."[9]

In arriving at a compelling justification, traditional appraisal canons will continue to serve archivists well. What they must do is apply these canons in a more rigorous, systematic, and documented way. A vital step in this process is a written analysis of controversial, complex, and significant appraisal questions.

The archivist needs to consider, in addition to traditional appraisal criteria, other factors in his assessment. One is an analysis of the extent to which documentation in print has devalued the information in the archival record. T.R. Schellenberg took note of this devaluation some twenty-four years ago when he wrote, "The volume of printed material is so great" that it is indeed questionable whether scholars would use and governments would be justified in preserving "any but a very small proportion of the unpublished public record."[10] Today, the bureaucratic process is amply documented with narrative and statistical reports, budgets and audits, investigations and hearings, and other documentation, much if not most of which finds its way into print. The archivist, then, must appraise his documentation not only in an interinstitutional context but also in a larger information context. More than ever, archivists, in their appraisal analysis, must know intimately the associated printed record held by libraries. This is not to suggest that archivists may passively allow librarians to make decisions for them, or otherwise do their job, but rather that they make librarians their partners in compiling and preserving the documentary record.

Another factor often overlooked in appraisal is the value of one set of records as a substitute for another set that is unavailable for preservation. A case in point are the records of American business enterprise. It is becoming increasingly clear that corporations, by and large, are not going to preserve a useful historical record—but governmental archives might. Activities such as the administration of justice, incorporation, licensing and regulation, taxation, the protection of labor and the consumer, and the promotion of business and economic activity produce enormous and comprehensive bodies of business and economic data that may provide a partial substitute for corporate documentation.[11]

A critical factor in a more disciplined appraisal process is a fiscal assessment of the cost of accessioning, organizing, and preserving the record. Archivists must learn to attach a price tag to their appraisal decisions. But how are they to arrive at a price? Only recently have archivists given any attention to measuring and analyzing these costs. A major cost, of course, is processing. Two recent studies claim that the cost of putting personal papers on the shelves may be between 32 and 88 dollars a cubic foot.[12] Even the higher figure of this estimate may be low when very complex collections are being processed. The price tag must also reflect conservation needs, which, in many cases, should include the cost of preservation microfilming. There are, in addition, long-term storage costs. A fiscal note should be an essential element of an appraisal report, but how relevant is such a note when certain considerations—research significance, institutional mission, or executive fiat—make accessioning mandatory? In such cases, the fiscal assessment is absolutely essential to the planning and budgeting process, and the price tag becomes even more relevant and important.

Both the traditional appraisal criteria and these other factors should be applied to the whole range of the historical record—photographs, sound recordings, television news footage, posters, handbills, and other ephemera. Even more than traditional paper records, the selection, intellectual control, and physical preservation of these materials make enormous demands on the archivist's resources. For example, out of the continuous television news coverage of a given community, what information merits preservation? What should a university archivist do with the masses of unidentified and unmanaged photographs transferred annually from the public relations office? Will identification and detailed processing of this material jeopardize the long-term preservation of, and access to, more vital university records? And does the preservation of these photographs in toto skew the historical record by placing too much emphasis on football and college presidents and too little on the longitudinal documentation of the institution?

Deaccessioning

Another application of this appraisal process is the third element in collection management: deaccessioning. A systematic and continuing procedure for reappraising and deaccessioning records is essential for good collection management. All archives have collections that by any reasonable appraisal standard would not be accessioned today—collections that are redundant, fragmentary, or otherwise without redeeming informational content. Some were acquired through archival passivity; some through an indiscriminate collection program; and some for donor relations. All were acquired in hopes that a more leisurely and thoughtful appraisal would be forthcoming. Unfortunately, to use Leonard Rapport's words, time has "burnished these records with a patina of permanence." We now publish information about them in our finding aids, and thus help to establish them as legitimate collections.[13]

Deaccessioning is not a novel strategy to archivists' museum and library allies, although they have been timid in its application. And there are good reasons for their timidity: it is a perilous business. There is so little guidance: no literature, no previous practice. As David Stam recently pointed out in his article, "Prove All Things: Hold Fast That Which Is Good," this is an area fraught with hostile emotion that tends to pit—to metaphrase—the true "archophile" against the corrupt "archophilistine."[14] The perils seem much greater for private than for public archives; former custodians of the latter often wonder why the records were preserved in the first place. There is the fear, though, that one incensed donor, proclaiming that valuable records have been destroyed, will put in jeopardy the whole collecting program—both for papers and money. The real peril of deaccessioning, however, is that fashion and ideology could wipe out an important dimension of the historical record. More archivists saving more records in more places spreads the burden of preservation in a spatial sense, but different judgments about the value of records over time spreads this burden in a very important temporal way. Deaccessioning should take place in an interinstitutional context to assure that archivists do not all throw out the same kinds of collections. It is essential, too, that deaccessioning decisions be meticulously documented and that they reflect—as should all good appraisal decisions—collective judgment.

Deaccessioning need not be synonymous with destruction. Reuniting split collections is one variant, but archivists need to go beyond this simple and obvious step and identify those collections that are worthy of preservation but are grossly out of scope and negotiate a more suitable home for them. And if they are risk takers, archivists will consider the sale of items of little informational but of some financial value, such as the autographed document and the stock certificate. (There were no such marketable documents in Governor Kerner's files, because Ralph Newman, with the donor's permission, had removed them. How much better it would have been had the repository reaped the financial rewards from the sale of items such as the autographed letters from Lyndon Johnson and Adlai Stevenson!) Archivists need to develop a policy that deals with the ethical and other problems of disposal and yet provides a modest financial benefit for the repository. One thing is clear: donor agreements cannot become the dead hand of the past; they must provide some option for reappraisal and deaccessioning.

Deaccessioning is not for the custodial archivist. Rather, it is a creative and sophisticated act of reappraisal that will permit the refinement and strengthening of archival holdings. It allows archivists to replace records of lesser value with collections of more significance, and it prevents the imposition of imperfect and incomplete decisions of the past on the future. Deaccessioning must become an integral part of collection management.

Are such choices really so perilous? Certainly the age of abundance has greatly lessened the value of any single set of records; our documents may be unique, but very little of the information in them is unique. This fact greatly lessens the impact of individual appraisal decisions. In the Kerner case, for example, Franklin stressed the significance of a few seemingly routine documents concerning a free Negro in the antebellum South. Such documents from an age of scarcity indeed may have great value, but if such a population group existed as a recognized class today, we would have hundreds of cubic feet of social service records, television documentaries, and investigatory reports to document them, and much of this documentation would no doubt be edited and published under National Historical Publications and Records Commission (NHPRC) sponsorship.

Pre-Archival Control

A fourth element of collection management involves the prearchival management of records. The archivist must participate in decisions about how record systems are organized and stored before they come to a repository as historical documents.

As modern bureaucracies of all sorts—in government, business, universities—adopt modern records-management techniques for handling information, the decisions of their information managers on file organization, access systems, and storage mediums will either facilitate or complicate the work of archival preservation. Increasingly, archivists will be accessioning packaged information systems with built-in storage and retrieval capabilities, not isolated record series or collections. These systems may be familiar paper or microfilm files, records in electronic data storage, video tapes, and discs, or complex systems involving several of these components.

If the archivist can identify such systems and their custodians, and, when necessary, influence their organization, the technical standards they must meet, or the type of documentation needed to facilitate their future use, then it is likely that systems with historical value can later be transferred to archival custody with most of the cost of processing and preservation already paid.

Lacking such assistance, even at the simplest level of document transfer—microfilming—the archivist may waste scarce resources for records preservation. A sad example is much of the microfilming of court case files in hundreds of counties throughout the nation. Because archivists were not involved in decisions about the arrangement, production, processing, and storage of these microfilmed records, and because some state archival agencies have inadequate standards for micrographics applications and quality control, archivists are faced with a Hobson's choice: either they accession bulky records that will be expensive to preserve and store, or they accept microfilm that does not meet minimum archival standards. In such a situation, collection management calls for an ounce of preventive assistance.

For many archivists, the voluminous office files of politicians and government officials are an even more familiar case in point. With good file management, scheduling, and micrographics—the key elements of a records-management program—these papers would not be jamming storage areas and adding to the processing backlog. Fortunately, the sheer mass of congressional files is promoting better paperwork management. Recently, several congressional offices have adopted an automated information-management system in which incoming correspondence is microfilmed and indexed by name and subject, while outgoing letters are reduced to a compact set of computer-generated informational elements—canned responses. Without archival input, archivists risk management efficiency at the expense of losing the historical records; with it, they preserve the record and greatly reduce storage and processing costs.

Prearchival management is imperative if archivists are to accession such information products of high technology as machine-readable records. In many ways, these records are the collection manager's dream, offering a potential solution to several problems associated with the modern record, including storage and access. Traditional processing costs are greatly reduced with machine-readable records because they require no physical rearrangement, weeding, refoldering, or container listing. Most objectives of archival arrangement are built into the file and, if the file documentation is in good order, the finding aid already exists. These records possess great advantages for users. The information they contain can be rearranged, aggregated, compared, and subjected to statistical tests without the laborious tasks of sample selection, data collection, coding, and data entry.[15]

The problems of accessioning these records, however, are formidable. The medium is fragile, the documentation is often haphazard, and the technology is sophisticated beyond the training and sensibilities of most archivists. To bridge the gap between the potential advantages of these files and the problems associated with accessioning and preserving them requires that archivists collaborate with their fellow information specialists in records management and data processing.

A caveat: Archivists should resist the temptation to accession "prepackaged" records simply because they can do so economically. Smaller is not necessarily better. Just as the uncontrolled accessioning of political papers and university archives has recently biased the documentary record, so can the uncontrolled accessioning of packaged information systems bias the record in the future.

Record Volume Reduction

The fifth element of collection management is the use of technology and sampling methodology to retain information while reducing the bulk of records.

For some time, archivists have been using some of the simpler forms of information technology to reduce the volume of records. The capabilities of micrographics systems for data compaction and preservation are well-known. The staff of the New York State Archives estimates that, eventually, 80 to 90 percent of their holdings will be stored in a microform format.[16] Too many archival programs fail to use the systems and exercise the options available. With higher reduction ratios made possible by today's optics, storage capacity can be increased many-fold.

There are attractive alternatives to the traditional 35 millimeter format for many applications. Micrographics provide extremely low-density data compaction when compared to electronic data storage. For most archives, however, conversion of existing archival records to a machine-readable format, because of high costs, will remain a low records-storage priority.

What may have a high priority—if promise is borne out by performance—is an optical or digitally encoded disc system that stores and retrieves information by laser. Currently in a highly experimental stage, the laser system, if successful, may contribute more than any other technological development to better collection management, because it could solve two of archivists' three greatest problems—storage and permanence. An experimental system at the Public Archives of Canada (PAC), using a disc a little larger than a phonograph record, has a storage capacity equivalent to 108,000 video frames or 100 reels of microfilm. And just about any image can be stored in the system. The PAC experiment includes prints, paintings, drawings, photographs (both black and white and color), paper documents, posters, maps, and motion pictures.

In addition to data compaction, another virtue of the laser recording is its stability, which surpasses that of most means of writing on paper and all means of magnetic-tape recording. Its fidelity, color, and audio qualities are excellent. A third virtue is the accessibility of the information; the system provides almost instantaneous retrieval by random address. Finally, the discs are easily duplicated, providing wide availability of material.[17]

The compaction of data, whether on microfilm or in electronic data storage, is not always an affordable or even a wise collection-management strategy. There are other methods to reduce bulk without significantly impairing the research value of records. These methods were much on the minds of National Archives and Records Service (NARS) officials in 1981, when they were under court order to develop a retention plan for the massive files of the Federal Bureau of Investigation (FBI)—some 25 million cases totaling about 300,000 cubic feet and dating from 1939 to the present.[18] How does one even examine files of this magnitude for appraisal purposes? Their numerical organization suggested that statistical sampling might prove a useful tool. Further, such a methodology had worked for Michael S. Hindus and his colleagues in the appraisal and selective retention of the less voluminous records (a mere 35,000 cubic feet) of the Massachusetts Superior Court from 1859 to 1959. In this latter case, the project staff first considered archival storage; none was forthcoming. Microfilming had a prohibitive 1.05 million-dollar price tag, and computer coding was likewise out of the question for fiscal reasons. Statistical sampling seemed to work.[19]

Using the Hindus report as a conceptual model, the NARS task force selected a stratified sample of 1,800 cases from the 214 FBI file classifications, collected basic information from each case, and produced a computer-generated classification profile to assist them in assessing the research potential of each file classification. The task force's retention sample reduces the volume of the files by about 83 percent.

The Hindus report and the FBI case files appraisal project have given archivists two pioneering examples of how to reduce the bulk of records while preserving intrinsic research value. No future archivist can justifiably consign important data to the scrap heap because of its bulk without first carefully analyzing the applicability of systematic sampling for the appraisal and scheduling of that data. Indeed, complex and difficult as it may be for all archivists, the application of mathematical approaches to sampling, as Frank Boles has pointed out, is as "unavoidable to the curator of large twentieth-century collections as the leap from item by item cataloging to group description."[20]

If the National Endowment for the Humanities provides the funding, some social-scientists-cum-archivists will combine statistical sampling with compaction by electronic data storage. The Inter-University Consortium for Political and Social Research at Ann Arbor is requesting a grant to sample Bureau of Labor Statistics records on the income and expenditure activities of U.S. families from 1888 to 1936. Data from a stratified statistical sample will be put into a machine-readable data file. With a valid sample in hand, the archivist can replace 400 cubic feet of records with a reel or two of tape.[21]

Analysis and Planning

The first five elements of collection management have dealt largely with what and how archivists accession. The sixth deals with how archivists manage those accessions once in their custody—that is, the application of analysis and planning to basic archival procedures to enable archivists to make better choices in the use of limited resources. As a prerequisite to such analysis and planning, archivists need data about archival activities as well as methods to analyze and transform this data into usable information. They need to measure what they do, especially their rates of processing and reference services, and they must assign a realistic cost to their activities. This information is essential not only for appraisal purposes but also for planning and management of all archival functions.

Recent literature offers some promising beginnings in this badly neglected field. A Society of American Archivists (SAA) task force has drafted recommendations for standard statistical reporting for archives of all sorts; William Maher has done pioneering work in applying financial analysis to basic archival activities; and Thomas Wilsted has given archivists a specific case study in applying cost analysis to archival processing.[22] This type of analysis needs to be extended to other archival activities, particularly reference services, conservation, and micrographics. The tools for better measurement and analysis are here; the next step is to apply them routinely to archival practice.

The need for informed decision making, based on analytical planning, is especially urgent in the area called processing—in the control of collections through arrangement and description. Because this activity so often is unplanned, many large and complex collections go unattended while huge sums are invested in processing others to unnecessary and wasteful levels of detail. Although the methodology of arrangement and description— controlling collections at various levels—provides a marvelously efficient and flexible approach to records processing, archivists' rigid application of the methodology has produced the opposite result. Archivists must learn that the ideal level is not the same for all collections; for some, the series, subgroup, or even collection level will do quite nicely. And, even within a single collection, various components may best be controlled at different levels.

To apply these notions to concrete situations, archivists need documented procedures, such as the preparation of written processing plans for all but the smallest and simplest accessions. These plans, analogous to appraisal reports, should review and elaborate on appraisal assessments, with recommendations for further weeding and compaction; they should specify the appropriate level of organization and description, provide a conservation needs assessment, and determine the level and type of staffing required for the various steps in processing. Decisions in each of these areas should take into account the importance of the records, the extent and nature of their anticipated use, the difficulty of providing reference services at different levels of control, the serviceability of the original file order, and, finally, the costs of various levels of processing. The staff of the Massachusetts Institute of Technology Archives, in their recently issued processing manual and other writings, have given archivists a model for analysis and planning in arrangement and description.[23]

Planned use of resources also is essential in determining appropriate levels of conservation, not only within collections, but at the institutional level as well. At one time, an item-level conservation approach might have seemed ideal, but now it is as archaic as item-level description. Just as it was necessary to move to collection-level description, so archivists must find an appropriate balance between improving collective conservation conditions (both in terms of shelf storage and ambient climate) and the labor-intensive activities of deacidification and encapsulation. Clearly, there are some documents in every archives that require heroic preservation efforts because of their intrinsic value. For most deteriorating collections, however, microfilming is, at present, the appropriate conservation technique. Because mass microfilming is costly, archivists must take care in determining which collections deserve such treatment. Many can wait, particularly those whose value is unclear when compared to the cost of their preservation. Storing collections until their value is clear—that is, until it is time to reappraise them— thus becomes part of good conservation and collection-management practice.

Planning for processing and conservation activities are only two examples of how archivists can better manage their scarce and diminishing resources. They need to apply these concepts to the whole range of archival activities. Collection management also demands planning at still another, higher level. Archivists must make planning decisions about these various activities. For example, it may be better management to assign a staff member to work with the state's congressional delegation in Washington, D.C., to establish records-management programs than to have an archivist commence all accessioning and arrangement activities only after the papers have appeared on the loading dock. Such decisions require archivists to make value judgments, to make cost analyses, to think in nontraditional ways, and, above all, to make difficult choices.

The elements outlined in this chapter are not the whole of collection management; undoubtedly, there are others that deserve discussion and inclusion. There is, however, one primary notion inherent in all of these elements—the need to identify and evaluate alternative courses of action. For too long, archival practices have followed the dictates of conventional wisdom and unexamined habit. The preservation demands of the modern records make following such dictates increasingly costly in real dollars. These are the overt costs. What of the hidden costs? The cost of foregone opportunities? The sacrifices made in pursuing less effective alternatives? In choosing options, archivists need to evaluate these opportunity costs, as economists call them. Wise choices will enable archivists to operate on what is called the production frontier, where they make optimal use of limited resources for greatest output. Only on this frontier can archivists cope with the age of abundance.

Notes

1. *Otto Kerner, Jr., and Estate of Helena C. Kerner, Deceased, Otto Kerner, Jr., Executor, Petitioners* v. *Commissioner of Internal Revenue, Respondent,* U.S. Tax Court Docket no. 4686-73 (filed January 19, 1976). Trial transcript, p. 80; T.C. memo, 1976–12.

2. Ibid., Exhibit A ("Inventory of the Otto Kerner Papers"); the author's (F. Gerald Ham's) telephone communication with the staff of the Illinois State Historical Library, October 4, 1982.

3. *Kerner* v. *Commissioner of Internal Revenue*, Exhibit I ("Appraisal of the Papers and Records of Otto Kerner, Jr., by F. Gerald Ham").

4. Thomas Wilsted, "Computing the Total Cost of Archival Processing," *MARAC'S Dear Archivist . . . Practical Solutions to Archival Dilemmas* (Summer 1983): 2-3.

5. Ham's communication with the staff of the Illinois State Historical Library, October 4, 1982.

6. Jutta Reed-Scott, "Collection Management Strategies for Archivists," paper presented at the 1982 Society of American Archivists Annual Meeting, Boston, Massachusetts, October 19, 1982.

7. See "Survey of Archival Networks," *Midwestern Archivist* 6 (1982): 98-127.

8. James E. Fogerty, "Manuscripts Collecting in Archival Networks," Ibid., p. 135.

9. New York State Archives, "Records Appraisal in the New York State Archives" (unpublished draft), p. 10.

10. Theodore R. Schellenberg, "The Future of the Archival Profession," *American Archivist* 22 (January 1959): 54-55.

11. F. Gerald Ham, "Wisconsin: Governmental Archives in an Academic Environment,"*Government Publications Review* 8A (1981): 304.

12. Wilsted, "Computing the Total Cost," pp. 2-3; William J. Maher, "Measurement and Analysis of Processing Costs in Academic Archives," *College & Research Libraries* 43 (January 1982): 59-67.

13. Leonard Rapport, "No Grandfather Clause: Reappraising Accessioned Records," *American Archivist* 44 (Spring 1981): 144, 145. Reprinted in *Prologue* 13 (Spring 1981): 49-55.

14. David H. Stam, " 'Prove All Things: Hold Fast That Which Is Good,' Deaccessioning and Research Libraries," *College & Research Libraries* 43 (January 1982): 6.

15. Margaret L. Hedstrom, "Planning for a Machine-Readable Records Program," paper presented at the Annual Conference of National Association of State Archives and Records Administrators, Nashville, Tennessee, July 23, 1982, pp. 24-26.

16. New York State Archives, "Conservation Policies and Programs for the New York State Archives" (unpublished draft, January 1982), p. 15.

17. Public Archives of Canada, "The Video Disc as a Pilot Project of the Public Archives of Canada" (unpublished paper, 1980).

18. National Archives and Records Service and the Federal Bureau of Investigation, *Appraisal of the Records of the Federal Bureau of Investi-*

gation: A Report to Hon. Harold H. Green, United States District Court for the District of Columbia (2 vols.; Washington, D.C.: National Archives and Records Service, 1981), Summary.

19. Michael Stephen Hindus, Theodore M. Hammett, and Barbara M. Hobson, *The Files of the Massachusetts Superior Court, 1859-1959: An Analysis and a Plan for Action* (Boston: G.K. Hall, 1980), pp. 3-9.

20. Frank Boles, "Sampling in Archives," *American Archivist* 44 (Spring 1981): 130.

21. National Endowment for the Humanities Grant #RT 20344-83, "Family Life and Conditions in the United States, 1888-1936."

22. "Draft Recommendations for Reporting on Archives and Manuscripts Collection," *SAA Newsletter* (July 1982): 11-13; William J. Maher, "The Importance of Financial Analysis of Archival Programs," *Midwestern Archivist* (1978): 3-24; Maher, "Measurement and Analysis," pp. 59-67; Wilsted, "Computing the Total Cost."

23. Karen T. Lynch and Helen W. Slotkin, *Processing Manual for the Institute Archives Collections M.I.T. Libraries* (Cambridge, Mass.: 1981); Slotkin and Lynch, "An Analysis of Processing Procedures: The Adaptable Approach," *American Archivist* 45 (Spring 1982): 155-163.

Bibliography

Anderson, Harold P. "Business Archives: A Corporate Asset." *American Archivist* 45 (Summer 1982): 264-266.

Aronsson, Patricia. "Congressional Records as Archival Sources." *Government Publications Review* 8A (1981): 295-302.

Bakken, Douglas. "Corporate Archives Today." *American Archivist* 45 (Summer 1982): 279-286.

Bauer, G. Philip. *The Appraisal of Current and Recent Records*. Staff Information Circulars, no. 13. Reprint. Washington, D.C.: National Archives and Records Service, 1976.

Benedon, William. *Records Management*. Englewood Cliffs, N.J.: Prentice Hall, 1969.

Blegen, August H. *Records Management Step-by-Step*. Stamford, Conn.: Office Publications, Inc., 1965.

Blouin, Francis X., Jr. "A Perspective on the Appraisal of Business Records." *American Archivist* 42 (July 1979): 312-320.

Boles, Frank. "Sampling in Archives." *American Archivist* 44 (Spring 1981): 125-130.

Bolton, Herbert E. *Guide to Materials for the History of the United States in the Principal Archive of Mexico*. Washington, D.C.: Carnegie Institution, 1913.

Booms, Hans. "Gesellschaftsordnung: und Überlieferungsbildung: Zur Problematik archivarischer Quellenbewertung." *Archivalische Zeitschrift* 68 (1972). The abstract appears in *Der Archivar* 25, pt. 1, (1972): cols. 23-28.

Bowers, Fredson. *Bibliography & Modern Librarianship*. Berkeley: School of Librarianship, University of California, 1966.

Brichford, Maynard J. *Archives & Manuscripts: Appraisal & Accessioning*. Chicago: Society of American Archivists, 1977.

Brooks, Philip C. "Records Selection—A Cooperative Task." *Indian Archives* 7 (July-December 1953): 79-86.

―――. "The Selection of Records for Preservation." *American Archivist* 3 (October 1940): 221-234.

―――. *What Records Shall We Preserve?* Staff Information Paper 9. Reprint. Washington, D.C.: National Archives and Records Service, 1975.

Burke, Frank G. "The Future Course of Archival Theory in the United States." *American Archivist* 44 (Winter 1981): 40-46.

Chandler, Alfred D. "The Beginnings of 'Big Business' in American Industry." *Business History Review* 33 (Spring 1959): 1-30.

————. *Strategy and Structure: Chapters in the History of Industrial Enterprise*. Cambridge, Mass.: M.I.T. Press, 1962.

————. *The Visible Hand: The Managerial Revolution in America*. Cambridge, Mass.: Belknap Press, 1977.

Cochran, Thomas C. *Business in American Life*. New York: McGraw-Hill, 1972.

————. "The New York Committee on Business Records." *Journal of Economic History* 5 (May 1945): 60-64.

Cole, Arthur H. "Business Manuscripts: A Pressing Problem . . . the Accumulated Development of Unsolved Problems." *Journal of Economic History* 5 (May 1945): 43-59.

Collingridge, J.H. "The Selection of Archives for Permanent Preservation." *Archivum* 6 (1956): 25-35.

Commission on Organization of the Executive Branch of the Government. *Paperwork Management, Part I, in the United States Government, A Report to Congress*. Washington, D.C.: Government Printing Office, 1955.

Conference on the Research Use and Disposition of Senator's Papers. *Proceedings*. Edited by Richard A. Baker. Washington, D.C.: 1978.

Darter, Lewis J., Jr. "Records Appraisal: A Demanding Task." *Indian Archives* 18 (January-June 1969): 2-10.

Davis, Lance E., and North, Douglas C. *Institutional Change and American Economic Growth*. Cambridge, England: University Press, 1971.

Deaccession in Research Libraries, Papers Read at a Symposium Held at Brown University, June 11, 12, 1981. Providence: 1981.

Dollar, Charles. "Appraising Machine-Readable Records." *American Archivist* 41 (October 1978): 423-430.

"Draft Recommendations for Reporting on Archives and Manuscripts Collections." *SAA Newsletter* (July 1982): 11-13.

Eberhart, Richard. *Of Poetry and Poets*. Urbana: University of Illinois Press, 1979.

Edmunds, Henry E. "The Ford Motor Company Archives." *American Archivist* 15 (April 1952): 99-104.

Evans, Frank B.; Harrison, Donald F.; and Thompson, Edwin A. "A Basic Glossary for Archivists, Manuscript Curators, and Records Managers." *American Archivist* 37 (July 1974): 415-433.

Faust, Albert B. *Guide to the Materials for American History in Swiss and Austrian Archives*. Washington, D.C.: Carnegie Institution, 1916.

Fishbein, Meyer H. "Appraising Information in Machine Language Form." *American Archivist* 35 (January 1972): 35-43.

————. "A Viewpoint on Appraisal of National Records." *American Archivist* 33 (April 1970): 175-187.

Fogerty, James E. "Manuscripts Collecting in Archival Networks." *Midwestern Archivist* 6 (1982): 130-141.

Gondos, Victor, Jr. *J. Franklin Jameson and the Birth of the National Archives, 1906-1926.* Philadelphia: University of Pennsylvania Press, 1981.

Griffin, Mary Claire. *Records Management: A Modern Tool for Business.* Boston: Allyn and Bacon, 1964.

Ham, F. Gerald. "Wisconsin: Governmental Archives in an Academic Environment." *Government Publications Review* 8A (1981): 303-309.

Hindus, Michael Stephen; Hammett, Theodore M.; and Hobson, Barbara M. *The Files of the Massachusetts Superior Court, 1859-1959: An Analysis and a Plan for Action.* Boston: 1980.

Hower, Ralph M. *The Preservation of Business Records.* Boston: Business Historical Society, 1941.

————. "Problems and Opportunities in the Field of Business History." *Bulletin of the Business Historical Society* 15 (April 1941): 17-26.

Johnson, H. Thomas. "Management Accounting in an Early Multidivisional Organization: General Motors in the 1920s." *Business History Review* 52 (Winter 1978): 490-517.

Jones, H.G. *The Records of a Nation.* New York: Athenaeum, 1969.

Kahn, Gilbert, et al. *Progressive Filing and Records Management.* New York: McGraw-Hill, 1962.

Kahn, Herman. "Mr. Kahn's Comments." In *The Appraisal of Current and Recent Records,* by G. Philip Bauer, pp. 22-25. Washington, D.C.: National Archives and Records Service, 1976.

Kaiser, Lisa. "Selection of Statistical Primary Material." *Archivum* 6 (1956): 75-80.

Kromnow, Åke. *The Appraisal of Contemporary Records.* Washington, D.C.: General Services Administration, 1976. An edited version of this paper was published in *Archivum* 26 (1979): 45-54.

Lamb, W. Kaye. "The Fine Art of Destruction." In *Essays in Memory of Sir Hilary Jenkinson,* edited for the Society of Archivists by Albert E.J. Hollaender, pp. 50-56. Chichester, England: Moore and Tillyer, 1962.

Larson, Henrietta. *Guide to Business History.* Cambridge, Mass.: Harvard University Press, 1948.

Leahy, Emmett J. "Reduction of Public Records." *American Archivist* 3 (January 1940): 13-38.

Leahy, Emmett J., and Cameron, Christopher A. *Modern Records Management.* New York: McGraw-Hill, 1965.

Levy, Robert. "Inside Industry's Archives." *Duns Review* 117 (May 1981): 72-76.

Lewis, W. David, and Newton, Wesley P. *Delta: The History of an Airline*. Athens: University of Georgia Press, 1979.

The Libraries of the Stanford University, Collection Development Policy Statement, 1980. Stanford: Collection Development Office, Stanford University Libraries, 1981.

Loring, Augustus P. "Deaccession and the Board of Trustees." In *Deaccession in Research Libraries, Papers Read at a Symposium Held at Brown University, June 11, 12, 1981*, pp. 17-18. Providence: 1981.

Lovett, Robert W. "The Appraisal of Older Business Records." *American Archivist* 15 (April 1952): 231-239.

Lutzker, Michael A. "Max Weber and the Analysis of Modern Bureaucratic Organization: Notes Toward a Theory of Appraisal." *American Archivist* 45 (Spring 1982): 119-130.

Lynch, Karen T., and Slotkin, Helen W. *Processing Manual for the Institute Archives Collection M.I.T. Libraries*. Cambridge, Mass.: 1981.

Madan, Falconer. "Duplicity of Duplication." *Transactions of the Bibliographical Society*. 12 (1914): 15-24.

Maedke, Wilmer O.; Robek, Mary F.; and Brown, Gerald F. *Information and Records Management*. Beverly Hills, Calif.: Glencoe Press, 1974.

Maher, William J. "The Importance of Financial Analysis of Archival Programs." *Midwestern Archivist* (1978): 3-24.

McCorison, Marcus. "Effects of Deaccession on Rare Book and Special Collections Libraries." In *Deaccession in Research Libraries, Papers Read at a Symposium Held at Brown University, June 11, 12, 1981*, pp. 29-33. Providence:1981.

McCoy, Donald R. *The National Archives: America's Ministry of Documents, 1934-1968*. Chapel Hill: University of North Carolina Press, 1978.

Modell, Peter. "Books at Auction: The Art of Deaccessioning." *Wilson Library Bulletin* 56 (September 1981): 33-38.

Neill, Desmond. "Defending Duplicates: The Value of Variant Copies." *Wilson Library Bulletin* 56 (May 1982): 669-72.

Nikirk, Robert. "Deaccession and Donor Relations." In *Deaccession in Research Libraries, Papers Read at a Symposium Held at Brown University, June 11, 12, 1981*, pp. 34-37. Providence: 1981.

Nilsson, Nils. *Arkivkunskap*. Lund: Studentlitteratur, 1972.

Rapport, Leonard. "No Grandfather Clause: Reappraising Accessioned Records." *American Archivist* 44 (Spring 1981): 143-150.

"Report of the Ad Hoc Committee on Manuscripts Set Up by the American Historical Association in December 1948." *American Archivist* 14 (July 1951): 229-240.

A Report to Hon. Harold H. Green, United States District Court for the District of Columbia. 2 vols. Submitted by the National Archives and

Records Service and the Federal Bureau of Investigation, November 9, 1981. Washington, D.C.: National Archives and Records Service, 1981.

Robbins, Albert, ed. *American Literary Manuscripts*. 2d ed. Athens: University of Georgia Press, 1977.

Robertson, James A. *List of Documents in Spanish Archives Relating to the History of the United States*. Washington, D.C.: Carnegie Institution, 1910.

Schellenberg, Theodore R. *The Appraisal of Modern Public Records*. Bulletins of the National Archives, no. 8. Washington, D.C.: National Archives and Records Service, 1956.

————. "The Future of the Archival Profession." *American Archivist* 22 (January 1959): 49-58.

————. *Modern Archives: Principles and Techniques*. Chicago: University of Chicago Press, 1956.

Slotkin, Helen W., and Lynch, Karen T. "An Analysis of Processing Procedures: The Adaptable Approach." *American Archivist* 45 (Spring 1982): 155-163.

Smith, David R. "An Historical Look at Business Archives." *American Archivist* 45 (Summer 1982): 273-278.

Society of American Archivists. College and University Archives Committee. Subcommittee on Standards. *Guidelines for College and University Archives*. Chicago: Society of American Archivists, 1982.

Stam, David H. " 'Prove All Things: Hold Fast to That Which is Good,' Deaccessioning and Research Libraries." In *Deaccession in Research Libraries, Papers Read at a Symposium Held at Brown University, June 11, 12, 1981*, pp. 1-13. Providence: 1981. Published in revised form in *College & Research Libraries* 43 (January 1982): 5-13.

Steck, Larry, and Blouin, Francis X., Jr. "Hannah Lay and Company: Sampling the Records of a Century of Lumbering in Michigan." *American Archivist* 39 (January 1976):15-20.

Streit, Samuel. "Research Library Deaccessioning: Practical Considerations." *Wilson Library Bulletin* 56 (May 1982): 658-662.

"Survey of Archival Networks." *Midwestern Archivist* 6 (1982): 98-127.

Tanenbaum, Charles. "Deaccessioning and the Collector: I." In *Deaccession in Research Libraries, Papers Read at a Symposium Held at Brown University, June 11, 12, 1981*, pp. 47-50. Providence: 1981.

Traister, Daniel. "Goodbye to All That: A Case Study in Deaccessioning." *Wilson Library Bulletin* 56 (May 1982): 663-668.

Whitehill, Walter. *Independent Historical Societies*. Boston: Boston Athenaeum, 1962.

Wilsted, Thomas. "Computing the Total Cost of Archival Processing." *MARAC's Dear Archivist . . . Practical Solutions to Archival Dilemmas* (Summer 1983): 1-3.

Index

Academic Collections, x, 19–59, 105, 118–121, 126–131. *See also* Accessioning; Appraisal; Archives; Deaccessioning; Files; Institutional alliances; Records; Records management

Accessioning, 107, 133, 134, 136, 137, 140, 143

"The Accumulated Development of Unsolved Problems," Arthur Cole, 64

Act Concerning the Disposal of Records, 2

Ad Hoc Committee on Manuscripts, American Historical Association, 4

Administrators, 13, 24, 35, 97, 117, 121, 122, 123, 131; and cooperation with archivists, 6

American Antiquarian Society, ix

American Archivist, 6

American Broadcasting Company (ABC), 127

American Council of Learned Societies, 62

American Historical Association, 4, 61

American Library Association, 62

American Literary Manuscripts, 105

Anderson, Harold, 75

Appraisal, vii, ix, x, 1, 3, 11, 16, 69, 74, 76, 95, 107, 115, 117, 143; and business records, 61–79; and case studies, 16, 123–126; and deaccessioning, 123–126; disciplined, 136–138; of literary manuscripts, 113–115; and records management, 19–59

"The Appraisal of Older Business Records," Robert Lovett, 67

Appraisers, 9, 114, 115

Archives: and institutional alliances, 97, 98–100; practice and theory, ix, 1–18, 21, 82, 95–100; prearchival

control, 140–141. *See also* Academic collections; Accessioning; Appraisal; Institutional alliances; Literary manuscripts; Records; Records management

Archivists, 1–2, 3, 4, 5–6, 34, 65, 73, 75, 77; appraisal criteria, 7–8, 9–14, 16, 19–20, 21, 62–63, 83–84, 112, 113–115, 136–138; congressional collections, 83–84, 86, 92, 94–96, 98, 99; cooperation with administrators, 6; deaccessioning, 117, 119, 122–123, 125, 126, 129, 131, 139; records management, 133, 134–135, 140–141, 143, 144, 145

Archivum, 9

Arkivkunskap, 11

Aronsson, Patricia, x, 81–104

Arts of the Book Collection, Sterling Library, 119

Arundel, Kenneth Roberts, 109

Association of Records Managers and Administrators, 68

Atlantic Monthly, 109

Auction houses, 118, 119

Baker Library, Harvard, 63, 64, 66, 69, 120

Bakken, Douglas, 70

Bancroft Library, University of California, 117

"Basic Glossary," Society of American Archivists, 81

Basic Manual Series, Society of American Archivists, 15

Bauer, G. Philip, 6

Beinecke Library, Yale, 119

Bentley Historical Library, 69

Blouin, Francis X., Jr., x, 61–79

Bok, Derek, 129

Boles, Frank, 143

Books, rare, 122. *See also* Literary manuscripts

155